Of Earth and Sky

SPIRITUAL LESSONS FROM NATURE

Compiled by Thomas Becknell

Augsburg

MINNEAPOLIS

For my brother, John,
who seeks to live deliberately

OF EARTH AND SKY
Spiritual Lessons from Nature

Cover design by David Meyer
Book design by Michelle L. N. Cook
Illustrations by Fran M. Roen

Library of Congress Cataloging-in-Publication Data
Of earth and sky: spiritual lessons from nature / compiled by Thomas Becknell.
  p. cm.
  Includes bibliographical references and index.
  ISBN 0-8066-4260-2 (alk. paper)
BV4509.5 .O33 2001
242—dc21   2001022094

The paper used in this publication meets the minimum requirements of American National Standard for Information Sciences—Permanence of Paper for Printed Library Materials, ANSI Z329.48-1984.

Manufactured in Canada.   AF 9-4260

05   04   03   02   01   1   2   3   4   5   6   7   8   9   10

Table of Contents

Introduction: Consider Creation

"Let us spend one day as deliberately as Nature," urged Henry David Thoreau in the mid-nineteenth century. To the lives of quiet desperation all around him, he sought to bring nature's message of simplicity and purposeful living.

Nature, throughout the centuries, has provided constant instruction in virtuous living. Its simple wisdom has inspired some of the world's greatest religious teachings and moral philosophies. "Go to the ant," instructs the proverbs, "consider its ways and be wise!" (Proverbs 6:6). "Consider how the lilies grow," Jesus taught (Luke 12:27). Nature's instruction is accessible and available to all. "Who can guess how much firmness the sea-beaten rock has taught the fisherman?" observed Ralph Waldo Emerson; "how much industry and providence and affection we have caught from the pantomime of brutes."

Some Christians have been reluctant to consider creation as an instructor for living. Some have been averse to ecological issues and particularly suspicious of any kind of natural spirituality. Yet "Nature to a saint is sacramental," as Oswald Chambers once put it. "In every blossoming and in every withering of the earth, there is a real coming of God to us if we will simply use our starved imagination to realize it."

Today, as the environmental crisis deepens and our distance from the natural world widens, we are finding an even greater hunger for wisdom and direction in knowing how to live purposefully and meaningfully. There is a renewed interest in acquiring virtues for living. And while some feel that traditional sources of guidance have failed or no longer seem adequate, the clear, simple lessons of nature endure, translated into words by some of the world's finest writers.

Of Earth and Sky provides a rich collection of these natural gems of wisdom. This book is not so much about living in harmony with nature as it is about composing one's life according to the virtues that nature teaches. "What is the shape of my life?" asks Anne Morrow Lindbergh, who finds the answer in the design of simple seashells. "I would like to learn, or remember, how to live," writes Annie Dillard. "And I suspect that for me the way is like the weasel's." From nature's bounty comes a rich variety of natural metaphors and patterns for composing one's life. Lessons drawn from lizards, trees, caterpillars, camels, snakes, manatees, eagles, toads, brooks, etc., encourage us to use our imagination for living prudently, or with limits, or in anticipation of new beginnings.

These spiritual lessons are written by those who trust nature's instruction. They don't preach. "A saint is capable of talking about the world without any explicit reference to God," Thomas Merton reminds us, "and arouses a greater love of God than the observations of someone less holy, who has to strain himself to make an arbitrary connection."

Of Earth and Sky encourages meaningful connections between the inner life and the natural world. These are the expressions of those who don't strain for spiritual insight, but simply bear witness to what they see in nature. Their examples invite us to take the time to consider creation and to ponder its lessons. Consider the fringed gentian that will not bloom until summer's glory has passed and every other flower has faded—and take hope! Consider the tenacity of the bur oak, or the quiet endurance of the turtle, or the sheer joy of the cardinal. Consider the blind faith of a honeysuckle shoot and the secret life of salamanders. Consider the elegance of the great egret and the grace of an occasional osprey. Consider the simple miracle of a blade of grass. "If it were not for the outside world," wrote George MacDonald, "we should have no inside world to understand things by. Least of all could we understand God without these millions of sights and sounds and scents and motions weaving their endless harmonies."

Nature's instruction is clear and direct. These are the lessons of ancient virtues.

In the late Middle Ages, St. Thomas Aquinas created a list of seven virtues as a basic guide for living a good life. Aquinas combined the four classical virtues of prudence, temperance, justice, and fortitude—taught by Plato and later by Cicero—with the three Christian graces of faith, hope, and charity, taught by St. Paul. Seven has always been regarded as a sacred number, the number of completeness. Think of the seven days of creation, the seven wonders of the world, the seven seas, the seven churches of Asia, the seven hills of Rome, the seven last words of Christ, or the seven seals of the apocalypse. In these seven virtues, then, are embodied all the many virtues we yearn for in our world—patience and loyalty and tolerance and empathy and trustworthiness and self-discipline and cooperation, to name just a few.

What Aquinas provided was a synthesis of ancient knowledge and Christian understanding. It was an elegant framework that was intensely Christian and, at the same time, broadly humanistic.

Throughout the ages, many have perceived a wonderful symmetry to his seven virtues. The three theological, God-given virtues—faith, hope, and charity—are balanced by three humanistic virtues—temperance, fortitude, and justice. These paired virtues, in turn, direct various aspects of one's being: faith and temperance appeal to the reason, hope and fortitude appeal to the passions, charity and justice appeal to the will. Wisdom (or, prudence), then, is that connecting virtue, directing all the other virtues so that one's whole being—mind, heart, and soul—has integrity and unity of purpose. The virtuous person, in short, is directed both by a devotion to God and by a devotion toward others.

Of Earth and Sky encourages you to practice the virtues. At the end of each chapter are seven suggestions for practicing that particular virtue; but these are only suggestions, as the readings themselves will inspire many other applications to your spiritual practice. One way to use this book might be to assign a particular day of the week to one of the seven virtues.

The selections in this book may be read in any order. You might find them useful as guides for personal contemplation and reflection. They might serve as a resource for group discussions. You might find this book to be an ideal companion on a wilderness outing.

The writers featured here come from various walks of life. But all of them model one very practical way to a deeper spiritual life—they recorded what they saw and what they thought or felt in response to nature. They put it into words, calling attention to it. You need not be a nature writer to do this. Try keeping a notebook, a diary, or a journal of your observations and reflections. Bear witness to God's creation—to the beauty of earth and sky, and to the wonder of your own existence. It might change your life!

Song of the Sky Loom

O our mother the Earth, O our father the Sky,
Your children we are, and with tired backs
We bring you the gifts that you love.
Then weave for us a garment of brightness;
May the warp be the white light of morning,
May the weft be the red light of evening,
May the fringes be the falling rain,
May the border be the standing rainbow.
Thus weave for us a garment of brightness
That we may walk fittingly where birds sing,
That we may walk fittingly where the grass is green,
O our mother the Earth, O our father the Sky.

NATIVE AMERICAN SONG

Prudence

Nature's Instruction
for Living Deliberately

IN A WORLD OF OVERNIGHT FORTUNES AND INSTANT ACCESS, who wants to be prudent? Prudent people avoid risk, don't they? The fiscally prudent seem cautious, and the politically prudent appear dull. Why, then, should prudence appeal?

What the ancient Romans called prudence, the Greeks called practical wisdom. Living prudently, for them, did not mean fearing risk. Rather, prudence is all about making wise choices. Of all the ancient virtues, prudence was considered primary—the prerequisite for living courageously or justly or temperately.

Practical wisdom, or prudence, is really the art of composing one's life. Prudence directs one, first, to find a worthy purpose in living, then serves to guide all of one's actions in the light of that purpose. Prudence enables one to live deliberately. A prudent person is one who knows what needs to be done. A prudent person makes decisions confidently, and can justify those decisions in light of a clearly established goal.

Centuries before the Greeks and Romans, the Old Testament proverbs were instructing its readers to get wisdom and prudence above anything else. Solomon, to whom most of those wise sayings were attributed, had not sought wealth, honor, long life, or victory over his enemies. As a result, God granted his request for wisdom, giving him not only unparalleled prudence, but also unsurpassed wealth and prestige. "The wisdom of the prudent," counseled Solomon, "is to give thought to their ways" (Proverbs 14:8). In contrast, those who lack prudence—the simple, the foolish, the thoughtless, the undisciplined, the unreliable—will inevitably fail. "You who are simple," he declared, "gain prudence" (Proverbs 8:5).

In the mid-nineteenth century, the American sage Ralph Waldo Emerson admonished: "Nature punishes any neglect of prudence." Emerson had been seeking to understand the wisdom of nature and its ministry to humanity. Prudence, he discovered, was a vital part of nature's instruction: "Prudence does not go behind nature and ask whence it is. It takes the laws of the world, whereby man's being is conditioned, as they are, and keeps these laws, that it may enjoy their proper good."

Today, some unprecedented environmental changes are forcing us to come to terms with a worldwide lack of prudence. The ominous beginnings of global warming, the thinning of earth's protective ozone, and the silent disappearance of thousands of species each year are the consequences of our going behind nature and not respecting its laws. We have used nature for our own ends rather than wisely for the good of all. We have not acted as good stewards of the earth.

Prudence, from the perspective of environmental stewardship, begins with understanding the complex interconnectedness of all life. We can never do just one thing to the environment, ecologists tell us. All our actions affect the web of life, which in turn affects us. Environmental prudence recognizes that we are all in this together, that what is good for an ecosystem is ultimately good for human life.

While ecologists can help us to understand and to respect Nature's laws, the writers in this chapter help us to see Nature's instruction for living, or as Thomas Aquinas described prudence, a right way of doing things *(Summa Theologica)*. Unlike the plants and the animals, humans have choice. "We can live any way we want," Annie Dillard reminds us. What Nature provides us are not models for choosing, but models of *being*—vibrant examples of things living as they were meant to live.

"I would like to live as I should, as the weasel lives as he should," writes Dillard. From the weasel, she learned "to stalk your calling in a certain skilled and supple way." Father Carlos Valles found wisdom through an ordinary caterpillar's "being fully and genuinely what it is now, not by trying to be what it is not." And a tiger beetle taught biologist John Janovy to understand the importance of finding the correct approach to living and acting.

Throughout the centuries, people of all cultures have turned to nature for this sort of wisdom. Sometimes that wisdom has been distilled and passed on in the form of a proverb. "A prudent man does not make his goat his gardener," says a Hungarian proverb. "Although it rains," advises a Malay saying, "cast not away the watering pot." And Jesus taught, "Be as shrewd as snakes and as innocent as doves" (Matthew 10:16).

Technology and contemporary lifestyles seem to distance us from the natural world and to cut us off from this traditional source of wisdom. Yet Nature's wisdom remains. The following selections can serve to reconnect us to this vital source of wisdom, showing us how Nature instructs us in living deliberately and purposefully.

Earth Teach Me
(A Ute Prayer)

Earth teach me stillness
    As the grasses are stilled with light.
Earth teach me suffering
    As old stones suffer with memory.
Earth teach me humility
    As blossoms are humble with beginning.
Earth teach me caring
    As the mother who secures her young.
Earth teach me courage
    As the tree which stands all alone.
Earth teach me limitation
    As the ant which crawls on the ground.
Earth teach me freedom
    As the eagle which soars in the sky.
Earth teach me resignation
    As the leaves which die in the fall.
Earth teach me regeneration
    As the seed which rises in the spring.
Earth teach me to forget myself
    As melted snow forgets its life.
Earth teach me to remember kindness
    As dry fields weep with rain.

Nancy Wood

The Utes lost most of their ancient homeland in the mid-nineteenth century when gold was discovered in Colorado. Today, the Northern Utes make their home on the Uintah and Ouray Indian Reservation in northeastern Utah, and the Southern Utes in southwestern Colorado. In 1976, Nancy Wood was commissioned to compose a musical work honoring the Utes, *War Cry on a Prayer Feather,* in which this prayer appears. Nancy Wood is the author of numerous works on Native American life and culture.

The Wisdom of the Caterpillar

We do not change by trying to be what we are not, but by being fully what we are. This is the secret. We do not change by looking at the future, but by living the present. When I am fully and generously all that I can and want to be in the present moment, I begin to feel inwardly ready to pass on to the next moment; when I am all I can be now, I spontaneously and obviously begin to be what I am to be next. The fullness of the present leads up by itself into the newness of the future. Today flowers into tomorrow when it is fully today, not when it pretends to be already tomorrow in impatient anticipation and undue haste. Thus change takes place precisely by not worrying about it, by not trying forcibly to bring it about, by not imposing it, by not seeking it. Let me be fully what I am today, and I shall wake up to a new world tomorrow.

An example: We know that a caterpillar turns into a chrysalis, and a chrysalis into a butterfly, which is a nature lesson of a wonderful change. Now, the caterpillar does not turn into a butterfly by *trying* to be a butterfly, by planning, scheming, endeavoring, or in any way contriving to be changed into a butterfly with colored wings and flying antennae. If it were to do that (as a man would surely do if he were in its place) it would only ruin its chances and spoil its future. A caterpillar becomes a butterfly by being a good, honest, healthy, reliable caterpillar; that is, by being fully and genuinely what it is now, not by trying to be what it is not. The better the caterpillar, the better the butterfly. The stronger the present, the brighter the future. The way for me to learn to fly one day is to walk firmly with my feet on the ground today. Nothing is achieved by dreaming and longing and craving and crying. Only by being fully what I am today can I get ready to be fully tomorrow what I can be tomorrow. My present stage fully lived is the best preparation for the next one. That is the wisdom of the caterpillar, and why it moves around contentedly at its leisurely pace. It trusts nature and it befriends time. It enjoys life crawling among leaves and branches, as one day it will enjoy life flying from flower to flower in the open sky. That is nature's kingdom.

CARLOS G. VALLES

Born in 1925, Carlos G. Valles is Father Valesa, a Spanish Jesuit who has worked in India for nearly forty years. He is the author of numerous books in Indian languages and in English.

Wisdom from Thorns and Nettles

"I went by the field of the slothful, and by the vineyard of the man void of under-standing," says Solomon; "I saw, and considered it well: I looked upon it, and received instruction." Whatever you see, take care to consider it well, and you will not see it in vain. You shall find books and sermons everywhere, in the land and in the sea, in the earth and in the skies, and you shall learn from every living beast, and bird, and fish, and insect, and from every useful or useless plant that springs out of the ground.

We may also gather rare lessons from things that we do not like. I am sure that Solomon did not in the least degree admire the thorns and the nettles that covered the face of the vineyard, but he nevertheless found instruction in them. Many are stung by nettles, but few are taught by them. Some . . . are hurt by briars, but here is one who was improved by them. Wisdom has a way of gathering grapes of thorns and figs of nettles, and she distills good from herbs which in themselves are noi-some and evil. Do not fret, therefore, over thorns, but get good out of them. Do not begin stinging yourself with nettles; grip them firmly, and then use them for your soul's health. Trials and troubles, worries and turmoils, little frets and little disappointments, may all help you if you will. Like Solomon, see and consider them well—look upon them, and receive instruction.

CHARLES H. SPURGEON

Charles Haddon Spurgeon (1834–92) was the most popular Baptist preacher in Victorian England. His sermons were known for their humor, common sense, and directness. He drew vast crowds to Exeter Hall, the Surrey Gardens Music Hall, and later to the Metropolitan Tabernacle, which he had specially constructed to seat 6,000. Spurgeon's first published sermon, delivered when he was only 20 years old, was "Harvest Time." In his preaching and writing, Spurgeon was particularly fond of turning to nature to illus-trate his points.

The Shape of My Life

The shell in my hand is deserted. It once housed a whelk, a snail-like creature, and then temporarily, after the death of the first occupant, a little hermit crab, who has run away, leaving his tracks behind him like a delicate vine on the sand. He ran away, and left me his shell. It was once a protection to him. I turn the shell in my hand, gazing into the wide open door from which he made his exit. Had it become an encumbrance? Why did he run away? Did he hope to find a better home, a better mode of living? I too have run away, I realize, I have shed the shell of my life, for these few weeks of vacation.

But his shell—it is simple; it is bare, it is beautiful. Small, only the size of my thumb, its architecture is perfect, down to the finest detail. Its shape, swelling like a pear in the center, winds in a gentle spiral to the pointed apex. Its color, dull gold, is whitened by a wash of salt from the sea. Each whorl, each faint knob, each criss-cross vein in its egg-shell texture, is as clearly defined as on the day of creation. My eye follows with delight the outer circumference of that diminutive winding stair-case up which this tenant used to travel.

My shell is not like this, I think. How untidy it has become! Blurred with moss, knobby with barnacles, its shape is hardly recognizable any more. Surely, it had a shape once. It has a shape still in my mind. What is the shape of my life?

ANNE MORROW LINDBERGH

Born into a prominent family, Anne Morrow Lindbergh (1906–2001) was educated at Smith College and married to aviator Charles Lindbergh. Flying together, she and Charles were sometimes referred to as "the lone eagle and his mate." The kidnapping and murder of their two-year-old son in 1932 brought her considerable anguish and painful publicity. This selection comes from her most popular book, *A Gift from the Sea*.

Small Wise Creatures

Four things on earth are small,
yet they are extremely wise:

Ants are creatures of little strength,
yet they store up their food in the summer;

Coneys are creatures of little power,
yet they make their home in the crags;

Locusts have no king,
yet they advance together in ranks;

A lizard can be caught with the hand,
yet it is found in kings' palaces.

PROVERBS 30:24-28

While many of the Proverbs are associated with the wise king, Solomon, these particular sayings are ascribed to Agur, son of Jakeh, an oracle. These are four lessons from nature in practical wisdom: small creatures overcoming their limitations and vulnerabilities through preparation (ants), position (coneys, or marmots), cooperation (locusts), and audacity (lizard).

On Seeing a Wild Bird

Beautiful symbol of a freer life,
Knowing no purpose, and yet true to one;
Would I could learn thy wisdom, I who run
This way and that, striving against my strife.

No fancy vague, no object half unknown,
Diverts thee from thyself. By stops and starts
I live the while by little broken parts.

A thousand lives—not one of all, my own.
Thou sing'st thy full heart out, and low or high
Flyest at pleasure; who of us can say
He lives his inmost self e'en for a day,
And does the thing he would? alas, not I.

ALICE CARY

Alice Cary (1820–71), the fourth of nine children, was raised on a farm in Ohio where life was harsh and books scarce. But she and her younger sister, Phoebe, maintained a passion for writing poetry, and in 1849 published a volume of their poems together. The following year, the sisters moved to New York where they shared a home for the rest of their lives, dying within months of each other. Alice's poetry was especially admired by the literary establishment of her time. John Greenleaf Whittier paid tribute to her in his poem "The Singer." Alice Cary's poems project a strong moral tone, and frequently draw their inspiration from nature.

Nature's Ministry

All things with which we deal, preach to us. What is a farm but a mute gospel? The chaff and the wheat, weeds and plants, blight, rain, insects, sun,—it is a sacred emblem from the first furrow of spring to the last stack which the snow of winter overtakes in the fields. But the sailor, the shepherd, the miner, the merchant, in their several resorts, have each an experience precisely parallel, and leading to the same conclusion: because all organizations are radically alike. Nor can it be doubted that this moral sentiment which thus scents the air, grows in the grain, and impregnates the waters of the world, is caught by man and sinks into his soul. The moral influence of nature upon every individual is that amount of truth which it illustrates to him. Who can estimate this? Who can guess how much firmness the sea-beaten rock has taught the fisherman? how much tranquillity has been reflected to man from the azure sky, over whose unspotted deeps the winds forevermore drive flocks of stormy clouds, and leave no wrinkle or stain? how much industry and providence and affection we have caught from the pantomime of brutes?

RALPH WALDO EMERSON

Ralph Waldo Emerson (1803–82) descended from a long line of Unitarian ministers, and was himself ordained at the age of 26. Three years later, he left the ministry to pursue a career of lecturing and writing. He settled in Concord, Massachusetts, forming friendships with other great writers and thinkers, including Henry David Thoreau, Nathaniel Hawthorne, Bronson and Louisa May Alcott, and Margaret Fuller. Emerson's influence upon the romantic movement in America was profound, and his thoughts have made an indelible impact on the American mind.

Fulfillment

To climb a hill that hungers for the sky,
To dig my hands wrist deep in pregnant earth,
To watch a young bird, veering, learn to fly,
To give a still, stark poem shining birth.

To hear the rain drool, dimpling, down the drain
And splash with a wet giggle in the street,
To ramble in the twilight after supper,
And to count the pretty faces that you meet.

To ride to town on trolleys, crowded, teeming,
With joy and hurry and laughter and push and sweat—
Squeezed next a patent-leathered Negro dreaming
Of a wrinkled river and a minnow net.

To buy a paper from a breathless boy,
And read of kings and queens in foreign lands,
Hyperbole of romance and adventure,
All for a penny the color of my hand.

To lean against a strong tree's bosom, sentient
And hushed before the silent prayer it breathes,
To melt the still snow with my seething body
And kiss the warm earth tremulous underneath.

Ah, life, to let your stabbing beauty pierce me
And wound me like we did the studded Christ,
To grapple with you, loving you too fiercely,
And to die bleeding—consummate with Life!

HELENE JOHNSON

Helene Johnson (1907–95) was one of the youngest writers of the Harlem Renaissance and a cousin to the late Dorothy West. She authored a number of award-winning poems and belonged to the Fellowship for Reconciliation, a pacifist organization.

The Good Gardener

The good gardener commonly borrows his methods, if not his goals, from nature
herself. For though nature doesn't seem to dictate in advance what we can do
in a place—we are free, in the same way evolution is, to try something completely new—in the end she will let us know what does and does not work.
She is above all a pragmatist, and so is the successful gardener.

By studying nature's ways and means, the gardener can find answers to
the questions. What is apt to work? What avails here? This seems to hold true
at many levels of specificity. In one particular patch of my vegetable garden—a
low, damp area— I failed with every crop I planted until I stopped to consider what
nature grew in a similar area nearby: briars. So I planted raspberries, which are of
course a cultivated kind of briar, and they have flourished. A trivial case, but it
shows how attentiveness to nature can help us to attune our desires with her ways.

The imitation of nature is of course the principle underlying organic gardening.
Organic gardeners have learned to mimic nature's own methods of building fertility
in the soil, controlling insect populations and disease, recycling nutrients. But the
practices we call "organic" are not themselves "natural" any more than the bird call of
a hunter is natural. They are more like man-made analogues of natural processes. But
they seem to work. And they at least suggest a way to approach other problems—
from a town's decision on what to do with a blown-down pine forest, to society's
choice among novel new technologies. In each case, there will be some alternatives
that align our needs and desires with nature's ways more closely than others.

It does seem that we do best in nature when we imitate her—when we learn to
think like running water, or a carrot, an aphid, a pine forest, or a compost pile.
That's probably because nature, after almost four billion years of trial-and-error
experience, has wide knowledge of what works in life. Surely we're better off
learning how to draw on her experience than trying to repeat it, if only because we
don't have that kind of time.

MICHAEL POLLAN

Born in 1955, Michael Pollan grew up on Long Island and was educated at Bennington
College, Oxford University, and Columbia University. He is currently a contributing editor for *Harper's*. In his book, *Second Nature: A Gardener's Education*, Pollan argues that a garden is a more promising way than wilderness for humans to relate to nature. Here, in this
lesson, what a gardener learns from nature can be applied to other aspects of one's life.

If We Surrendered to Earth's Intelligence

How surely gravity's law,
strong as an ocean current,
takes hold of even the smallest thing
and pulls it toward the heart of the world.

Each thing—
each stone, blossom, child—
is held in place.
Only we, in our arrogance,
push out beyond what we each belong to
for some empty freedom.

If we surrendered
to earth's intelligence
we could rise up rooted, like trees.

Instead we entangle ourselves
in knots of our own making
and struggle, lonely and confused.

So, like children, we begin again
to learn from the things,
because they are in God's heart;
they have never left him.

This is what the things can teach us:
to fall,
patiently to trust our heaviness.
Even a bird has to do that
before he can fly.

RAINER MARIA RILKE

Born in Prague, the German poet Rainer Maria Rilke (1875–1926) traveled widely throughout Europe. On a trip to Russia in 1899, he was inspired by the Christianity of Leo Tolstoy and the Russian peasants he met. This poem was written shortly after that trip.

Living Like Weasels

Weasel! I'd never seen one wild before. He was ten inches long, thin as a curve, a muscled ribbon, brown as fruitwood, soft-furred, alert. His face was fierce, small and pointed as a lizard's; he would have made a good arrowhead. There was just a dot of chin, maybe two brown hairs' worth, and then the pure white fur began that spread down his underside. He had two black eyes I didn't see, any more than you see a window.

The weasel was stunned into stillness as he was emerging from beneath an enormous shaggy wild rose bush four feet away. I was stunned into stillness twisted backward on the tree trunk. Our eyes locked, and someone threw away the key.

Our look was as if two lovers, or deadly enemies, met unexpectedly on an overgrown path when each had been thinking of something else: a clearing blow to the gut. It was also a bright blow to the brain, or a sudden beating of brains, with all the charge and intimate grate of rubbed balloons. It emptied our lungs. It felled the forest, moved the fields, and drained the pond; the world dismantled and tumbled into the black hole of eyes. If you and I looked at each other that way, our skulls would split and drop to our shoulders. But we don't. We keep our skulls. So.

❦

I would like to learn, or remember, how to live. I come to Hollins pond not so much to learn how to live as, frankly, to forget about it. That is, I don't think I can learn from a wild animal how to live in particular—shall I suck warm blood, hold my tail high, walk with my footprints precisely over the prints of my hands?—but I might learn something of mindlessness, something of the purity of living in the physical senses and the dignity of living without bias or motive. The weasel lives in necessity and we live in choice, hating necessity and dying at the last ignobly in its talons. I would like to live as I should, as the weasel lives as he should. And I suspect that for me the way is like the weasel's: open to time and death painlessly, noticing everything, remembering nothing, choosing the given with a fierce and pointed will.

❦

I missed my chance. I should have gone for the throat. I should have lunged for that streak of white under the weasel's chin and held on, held on through mud and into the wild rose, held on for a dearer life. We could live under the wild rose wild as weasels, mute and uncomprehending. I could very calmly go wild. I could live two days in the den, curled, leaning on mouse fur, sniffing bird bones, blinking, licking, breathing musk, my hair tangled in the roots of grasses. Down is a good place to go, where the mind is single. Down is out, out of your ever-loving mind and back to your careless senses. I remember muteness as a prolonged and giddy fast, where every moment is a feast of utterance received. Time and events are merely poured, unremarked, and ingested directly, like blood pulsed into my gut through a jugular vein. Could two live that way? Could two live under the wild rose, and explore by the pond, so that the smooth mind of each is as everywhere present to the other, and as received and as unchallenged, as falling snow?

We could, you know. We can live any way we want. People take vows of poverty, chastity, and obedience—even of silence—by choice. The thing is to stalk your calling in a certain skilled and supple way, to locate the most tender and live spot and plug into the pulse. This is yielding, not fighting. A weasel doesn't "attack" anything; a weasel lives as he's meant to, yielding at every moment to the perfect freedom of single necessity.

❦

I think it would be well, and proper, and obedient, and pure, to grasp your one necessity and not let it go, to dangle from it limp wherever it takes you. Then even death, where you're going no matter how you live, cannot you part. Seize it and let it seize you up aloft even, till your eyes burn out and drop; let your musky flesh fall off in shreds, and let your very bones unhinge and scatter, loosened over fields, over fields and woods, lightly, thoughtless, from any height at all, from as high as eagles.

ANNIE DILLARD

Born in 1945 in Pittsburgh, Annie Dillard won the Pulitzer Prize in 1975 for her first book of nature writing, *Pilgrim at Tinker Creek*. "Art is my interest," she once said; "mysticism my message, Christian mysticism." Among her popular books are *Holy the Firm* (1977), *Teaching a Stone to Talk* (1982), *An American Childhood* (1987), *The Writing Life* (1989), and *For the Time Being* (2000). Annie Dillard currently lives in Connecticut.

Living as the Willow

I must receive my life as passively as the willow leaf that flutters over the brook. I must not be for myself, but God's work, and that is always good. I will wait the breezes patiently, and grow as they shall determine. My fate cannot but be grand so. We may live the life of a plant or an animal without living an animal life. This constant and universal content of the animal comes of resting quietly in God's palm. I feel as if I could at any time resign my life and the responsibility into God's hands, and become as innocent and free from care as a plant or stone.

HENRY DAVID THOREAU

When Henry David Thoreau (1817–62) set down these words in his journal on March 11, 1842, he was 24 years old and working in his father's pencil factory in Concord, Massachusetts. He had graduated from Harvard five years earlier and was still undecided about his career, having taught school for a short time and working as a handyman, a tutor, and later as a surveyor. On July 4, 1845, Thoreau embarked on his famous experiment to "live deliberately" in the woods around Walden Pond.

A Mouse in the Moonlight

Once when camped on a rocky point along the Canadian border with the moon at full and my tent pitched in the light of it, I was lying in my sleeping-bag, tent flaps open, studying the effect of pine needles etched against the sky. Suddenly I was aware of a slight rustle as though some small animal was trying to climb the silken roof of the tent. Then I saw that it was a mouse scrambling desperately up the edge of the side wall. For a moment it hesitated, then stepped backward, and I thought it surely must fall. Another wild scramble and it was on the ridge rope itself, tottering uncertainly back and forth. Then, to my amazement, the mouse launched itself out into space and slid down the smooth and shining surface of the tent to the ground below.

The action was repeated many times until the little animal became expert and reckless and lost no time between the climb back and the sheer abandon of its slide. Faster and faster it ran, intoxicated now by its new and thrilling experience; up along the edge straight toward the center of the ridge rope, a swift leap, belly down, legs spread wide to get the full effect of the exhilarating toboggan it had found, a slide of balloon silk straight to the needle-strewn ground below.

I watched the game for a long time. Eventually I stopped trying to count the slides and wondered at last how the mouse could possibly keep up its pace. As I lay there, I became convinced that it was enjoying itself hugely, that I was witnessing an activity which had no purpose but pleasure. I had seen many animals play in the moonlight—had watched a family of otters enjoying a slide into a deep pool, beaver playing a game of tag in a pond, squirrels chasing one another wildly through the silver-splashed tops of the pines. Under the magic spell of the moon, the mouse had acted no differently than the rest.

I thought as I lay there in my bag that, if nothing else, moonlight made animals and men forget for a little while the seriousness of living; that there were moments when life could be good and play the natural outlet for energy. I knew that if a man could abandon himself as my dear mouse had done and slide down the face of the earth in the moonlight once a month—or once a year, perhaps—it would be good for his soul.

SIGURD F. OLSON

The son of a Baptist minister, Sigurd F. Olson (1899–1982) devoted his life to wilderness preservation. He made his home in Ely, Minnesota, near his beloved Boundary Waters Canoe Area Wilderness.

Nature's Great Circle

You have noticed that everything an Indian does is in a circle, and that is because the Power of the World always works in circles, and everything tries to be round. In the old days when we were a strong and happy people, all our power came to us from the sacred hoop of the nation, and so long as the hoop was unbroken, the people flourished. The flowering tree was the living center of the  hoop, and the circle of the four quarters nourished it. The east gave peace and light, the south gave warmth, the west gave rain, and the north with its cold and mighty wind gave strength and endurance. This knowledge came to us from the outer world with our religion. Everything the Power of the World does is done in a circle. The sky is round, and I have heart that the earth is round like a ball, and so are all the stars. The wind, in its greatest power, whirls. Birds make their nests in circles, for theirs is the same religion as ours. The sun comes forth and goes down again in a circle. The moon does the same, and both are round. Even the seasons form a great circle in their changing, and always come back again to where they were. The life of a man is a circle from childhood to childhood, and so it is in everything where power moves. Our tepees were round like the nests of birds, and these were always set in a circle, the nation's hoop, a nest of many nests, where the Great Spirit meant for us to hatch our children.

BLACK ELK

Black Elk (1863–1950) was an Oglala Lakota holy man who was born into a traditional Lakota world and witnessed its gradual destruction. In the 1880s, he traveled with Buffalo Bill's Wild West Show, and in 1890 survived the massacre at Wounded Knee. In 1904, Black Elk converted to Catholicism and served as a missionary to other Native Americans. In 1930, Black Elk was visited by the journalist John G. Neihardt, who translated the story of Black Elk's life in the very popular book, *Black Elk Speaks*.

Living Deliberately

It is highly improbable that we shall ever again lead what a Thoreau would be willing to call a "natural life." Moreover, since not every man has the temperament of a camper, it is not likely that most people will take even periodically to the woods. But there are other ways in which even the urban dweller not fortunate enough to have his country home can remain aware, at least in the important back of his mind, of the fact that his true place is somewhere in nature.

The more complicated life becomes, the more important is the part that symbols play, and all the arts, including the arts of architecture and decoration, are the products of symbolic acts. To plant a garden, a window box, or even to cultivate a house plant is to perform a sort of ritual and thereby to acknowledge, even in the middle of a city, one's awareness that our real kinship is with life, not with mechanism. To hang a picture or to choose a design or a color may be, only a little more remotely, the same thing.

It may be upon such rituals that our fate will ultimately depend. Organisms are rebellious, individual, and self-determining. It is the machine which is manageable and obedient, which always does the expected and behaves as it is told to behave. You can plan for it as you cannot plan for anything which is endowed with a life of its own, because nothing which is alive ever wholly surrenders its liberties. Man will not surrender his unless he forgets that he too belongs among living things.

JOSEPH WOOD KRUTCH

Joseph Wood Krutch (1893–1970) became one of America's most prolific nature writers and highly-sought editor and mentor of other nature writers. Early in the twentieth century, he served as a reporter at the Scopes trial and taught English at Columbia University. Among his many well-known books are *The Twelve Seasons* (1949), *The Desert Year* (1952), *The Voice of the Desert* (1955), and *More Lives Than One* (1962).

Tigers and Toads

Tiger beetles have a certain reputation among those who know them only slightly, or have tried to catch them. The reputation is one of speed coupled with almost purposeful behavior, a sort of halting run, that makes a tiger beetle simply very hard to catch by normal means. One does not walk up to a tiger beetle and pick it up. Nor does one easily sweep up a tiger beetle with a net skimmed over the white blistering surface of Arthur Bay dunes. No, the way to catch a tiger beetle is to act like a toad. The way to catch speed, grace, beauty, elegance, is to act dumb, slow, ugly, ungainly? No, patient. The Rocky Mountain toad is a packet of patience. But there is something deeper here: Patience is nothing more than the correct approach, and therein lies the lesson of this beauty and this beast. The correct approach, regardless of outward appearance, is the one attribute that will always net the prey.

And into how many other circumstances can this rule be inserted? Into many, is the answer. On many barren dunes will the correct approach capture beauty and grace. All one has to do is develop the approach. Now there is a challenge! We are not always born with it, latent, awaiting only time, warmth, and water, as are those black pollywogs out near Arthur Bay. But we can plan for the correct approach. We can develop the correct approach on purpose, or teach it to others.

❧

I tested my limits one day, out on those white sands of Arthur Bay. I took upon myself the task of getting close to a tiger beetle. The idea that morning was to establish a photographic record of the tiger-toad relationship. That relationship would make a good subject for a charming lecture to some civic group. After all, Beauty and the Beast has stood the test of time; and tigers and toads is a sort of beauty and the beast kind of tale. But the tiger proved more elusive than the toad, the beauty more elusive than the beast, until, of course, I acted like a beast. So here is a short biology lesson for those of you who will never crawl around in the Arthur Bay sand: In order to photograph the tiger you must be patient and slow, always giving the beauty time to adjust to your presence. You must not all at once present too much of a difference from your surroundings. And, it helps immeasurably to get down on the same level as the beauty. With those simple techniques, the correct approach, you can come as close to beauty as your beastly desires want. I was too close for my lenses. I lay in the sand of Arthur Bay eye-to-eye with a tiger beetle,

and successfully resisted the temptation to eat it, sensing, somehow, that my tongue might not be as sticky as a toad's. I
stood then, to full posture, brushing away the sand,
and beauty flew away many yards. But my eyes had
adjusted and suddenly there were hundreds of
tiger beetles everywhere, ones I had not seen
before getting eye-to-eye with one.

I'm sure the recreational folks of Arthur Bay
saw me as different from themselves that day. And
I'm just as sure that my behavior required no great measure of courage. No, acting
like an animal to get close to an animal, acting like a plant to get close to an animal,
those are things biologists do. But still, the decision to act like a toad is a decision
not everyone would make, and furthermore, I would not make except on the sands
of some Arthur Bay. I don't crawl along city sidewalks. But I am very alert to that
tiger beetle beauty wherever it can be found. And I am very aware that there are
options, behavioral and cultural options, that will lead me to that beauty regardless
of the form that beauty takes.

The elegant experiment, is that not beauty? The clean glassware; the perfect
culture medium; the student who follows your best lecture with a most penetrating
question; your child making a decision that makes you, in turn, so proud; the wren
that actually uses the house you built; the title remembered from a hazy past but
plucked from a browser's library shelf; are those not also things of beauty? And do
those things not also require the correct approach, the correct frame of mind, the
purposeful circumstance that brings out not only their beauty, but also your own
willingness to see that beauty? Yes, to all those questions.

JOHN JANOVY, JR.

**Born in 1937, John Janovy, Jr., grew up in Oklahoma and is currently the Varner
Distinguished Professor of Biology at the University of Nebraska. His research around
Keith County in western Nebraska has inspired many books, such as** Keith County Journal
(1980), Yellow Legs **(1981),** On Becoming a Biologist **(1986),** Fields of Friendly Strife **(1988), and**
Vermilion Sea: A Naturalist's Journey in Baja California **(1992).**

To Think Like a Snake

Encounters with animals are a gold mine of interest because the more you learn about an animal, the more improbable it seems, and you realize suddenly that there is more than one way to skin a cat, more than one way to live a life. The characteristics possessed by humans—five senses, daylight vision, a certain moral compunction about eating relatives, a daily schedule, and nowhere near enough time to wait for a good storm—are facts that restrict the way humans live. But they do not necessarily impose any such limits on an animal's life. Rattlesnakes can see pictures drawn by heat. Toads can go underground without any more fuss than going to the grocery store and live a life that would be, for a human, the most exquisite, brutalizing torture, buried for years, deprived of every sense but touch.

Observing animals, you also learn that the categories that enrich human lives— self-righteousness, reflective thought, empathy, planning to a purpose—are utterly absent from the experiences of the animals, or at least that's what I am assuming from what I know about the structure of their brains. Snakes and toads have a primitive brain, hardwired for fear and the detection of prey, for sex, hunger, and thirst. We primates have that brain too, and on top of that, the layered accretions of the cerebral cortex. So I come the closest to thinking like a snake, to seeing the world through the brain of a toad, when my body reacts to a stimulus with terror or elation and leaves my conscious mind out of the process.

I study the issue: What was I thinking about when I was thinking with my reptilian precursor of a brain, when I was frightened by the snake and yowled, and leaped back, and froze? In the effort to remember, I reconstruct the sequence of events in my mind, and at the point where the snake buzzed, I find ... nothing. Nothing. No visual images. I don't even find a memory of the first sound of the rattle. No memory of jumping. A step off the trail toward the adobe bricks, a blank space (maybe a dark space), and then I'm ten feet behind where I was before, my shout echoing against the rock, my mind ablaze with interest in a snake that is still ripping off a buzz to terrify the world.

So maybe I know what it is like to think like a snake, because I know what it is like to think not at all—to act with no memory, with no decision, with no awareness, to do the appropriate thing at the appropriate time and nothing more.

KATHLEEN DEAN MOORE

Kathleen Dean Moore is a philosopher who also writes nature essays.

Everything That Is, Is Holy

A saint is capable of loving created things and enjoying the use of them and dealing with them in a perfectly simple, natural manner, making no formal references to God, drawing no attention to his own piety, and acting without any artificial rigidity at all. His gentleness and his sweetness are not pressed through his pores by the crushing restraint of a spiritual strait-jacket. They come from his direct docility to the light of truth and to the will of God. Hence a saint is capable of talking about the world without any explicit reference to God, in such a way that his statement gives greater glory to God and arouses a greater love of God than the observations of someone less holy, who has to strain himself to make an arbitrary connection between creatures and God through the medium of hackneyed analogies and metaphors that are so feeble that they make you think there is something the matter with religion.

The saint knows that the world and everything made by God is good, while those who are not saints either think that created things are unholy, or else they don't bother about the question one way or another because they are only interested in themselves.

THOMAS MERTON

The spiritual quest of Thomas Merton (1915–68) led him to join a Trappist monastery at Gethsemani in Kentucky. There he lived simply, took vows of silence, and composed his spiritual autobiography, *The Seven Storey Mountain*. His book was enormously popular, and was often compared to *The Confessions of St. Augustine*. His writings continue to appeal to spiritual readers of all faiths.

How to Live

The economy of nature, its checks and balances, its measurements of competing life—all this is its great marvel and has an ethic of its own. Live in Nature, and you will soon see that for all its non-human rhythm, it is no cave of pain. As I write I think of my beloved birds of the great beach, and of their beauty and their zest of living. And if there are fears, know also that Nature has its unexpected and unappreciated mercies.

Whatever attitude to human existence you fashion for yourself, know that it is valid only if it be the shadow of an attitude to Nature. A human life, so often likened to a spectacle upon a stage, is more justly a ritual. The ancient values of dignity, beauty, and poetry which sustain it are of Nature's inspiration; they are born of the mystery and beauty of the world. Do no dishonor to the earth lest you dishonor the spirit of man. Hold your hands out over the earth as over a flame. To all who loved her, who open to her the doors of their veins, she gives of her strength, sustaining them with her own measureless tremor of dark life.

HENRY BESTON

Henry Beston (1888–1968) grew up in Massachusetts, graduated from Harvard with degrees in English, and, like Ernest Hemingway, served as an ambulance driver in World War I. Although he had written a number of books, he was virtually unknown until the age of 40 when he published *The Outermost House,* his classic account of a year spent alone in a two-room house on the beach of Cape Cod. Beston said that his most important discovery in that experience was "that the creation is still going on, that the creative forces are as great and active today as they have ever been…. Creation is here and now."

Practicing the Virtue of Prudence

1. Following the example of Helene Johnson, make a list of all the specific actions that you associate with "fulfillment." Compose your list as a column, beginning each line as she does with a specific action, such as: "to climb," "to dig," "to watch," etc. Include those actions that you've never done, but think you would enjoy.

2. As she considers the shape of a seashell, Anne Morrow Lindbergh asks, "What is the shape of my life?" Create a simile for your own life by completing this sentence: "My life is like _____." The object you liken to your life can be a manufactured object, as well as a natural object: "My life is like a balsam fir, or an interstate highway, or a loaded gun," etc. One famous poem, for example, begins: "My life is like a weaving" in which God sees the upper side, and the poet the underside. Play with this simile, trying to unpack all the associations. Consider: is this a desirable shape for your life or one you would like to change?

3. By considering the example of the caterpillar, Carlos Valles concludes, "Only by being fully what I am today can I get ready to be fully tomorrow what I can be tomorrow." Consider one other example from nature that seems to be living fully and genuinely what it is. Consider what it would mean for you to live fully what you are in the moment, to be all you can be now. Try to live one day with that intentional awareness.

4. Play can be good for the soul, Sigurd F. Olson concludes after contemplating the mouse in the moonlight. Take Olson's suggestion: abandon yourself as the mouse had done, to an energetic night (or day or weekend) of play, forgetting for the time the seriousness of living.

5. Black Elk claims that "everything an Indian does is in a circle" because nature's pattern is a circle. The Western mind, however, often prefers the linear to the circular. Why? Make a list of all the ways your life is shaped by straight lines, squares and rectangles: the shape of your house, the grid patterns of our city streets, calendars, graphs, appointment books, classrooms, etc. Consider the ways in which a circle might provide a more desirable or a more natural pattern for activities, or for thinking about your life.

6. What would it be like to live like a weasel, as Annie Dillard suggests, "to stalk your calling in a certain skilled and supple way"? What would it be like to live as a willow, as Thoreau desires, "to wait the breezes patiently"? Use one of the similes from this chapter, or discover one of your own. Draw out the implications, for you, of living so intentionally.

7. Tend a garden.

Fortitude

Nature's Instruction
for Remaining Steadfast

IN THE DAYS OF THE ROMAN EMPIRE, when Christians were experiencing great persecution, the story was told of the martyrdom of a wealthy Roman woman, Perpetua, and her slave Felicitas. When the gladiator's sword struck Perpetua's neck, it hit bone; and as it did not kill her immediately, Perpetua reached up and shifted the hand of the clumsy gladiator to her throat.

Throughout the centuries, martyrdom has served as the ultimate expression of Christian fortitude. "The blood of the martyrs are the seeds of the church," said one of the early church fathers; for there was something powerfully inspiring about the courage with which these Christians faced death. Even the pagan Romans could distinguish between the physical courage of two gladiators competing and the moral courage of the Christians accepting death for the sake of their beliefs.

Most of us today are not likely to endure martyrdom. Yet our need for fortitude is as keen as ever. We live in a society which champions courage. We celebrate athletes and fighters, those with strong arms and quick guns, those who battle fires and cancer and hostile forces. And while much can be said for the raw stuff of courage and for the daring displays of the heroes who have it, fortitude is a different sort of courage.

Fortitude is a courage of the heart, not of the glands. Its appearance is often quieter and less conspicuous than outward displays of bravery. The inner conflicts of the heart, according to the poet Emily Dickinson—who daily practiced fortitude—are far more gallant, though usually unnoticed:

> To fight aloud, is very brave—
> But gallanter, I know
> Who charge within the bosom
> The Cavalry of Woe—
>
> Who win, and nations do not see—
> Who fall—and none observe—
> (Poems of Emily Dickinson)

Fortitude is not reckless or foolhardy. Nor is it merely a bull-headed tenacity. It is a steadfastness that is informed by prudence. Fortitude requires commitment to some larger cause that gives one's life purpose and meaning. As St. Ambrose once put it, "Fortitude does not trust itself." In the case of the martyrs, that guiding cause was the kingdom of Christ. In the case of Emily Dickinson, who endured a lifetime of rejection, it was a commitment to her poetic vision and to her God-given talent as an artist.

Among the many public figures of the twentieth century who demonstrated the virtue of fortitude, we might think of Martin Luther King, Jr., Mohandas Gandhi, Mother Teresa, or Nelson Mandela. These individuals were guided in their steadfastness by a clear vision of a world without injustice and poverty and oppression.

But fortitude is practiced just as vigorously in the lives of ordinary people. Its struggles and its triumphs, as the poem suggests, usually go unobserved. Consider parents who patiently care for an autistic child, year after year, at great social and emotional cost. Consider a young student who refuses the perfect opportunity to cheat, and accepts instead a lower grade. Consider a teenager who endures taunts and social rejection because she stands up for what she knows is right. Consider a couple who maintains their commitment to each other, even when the thrill of the relationship has faded. Consider those who experience loss of health or homes or friendship, and keep going on. Sometimes even to live requires fortitude.

The fortitude we see in others does inspire us. But how can Nature instruct us in fortitude? Some of the lessons we have drawn from Nature have been simply misleading: the lion does not show us courage; the fox is not particularly cunning.

Simone Weil, the great French philosopher, once claimed that "to be rooted is perhaps the most important and least recognized need of the human soul" *(The Need for Roots)*. Rootedness provides a wonderful, gripping image of fortitude. "I fortify myself with these: the calm assurances of trees," says Clinton Scollard. A tree—particularly the hearty sort of tree that Sarah Orne Jewett describes growing out of "bare stony hills where you can't seem to see a wheel-barrowful o' good earth"—can strengthen the heart. "Have you ever imagined yourself to be a tree?" asked the late forester, Richard St. Barbe Baker. "Hold that sprouting idea for a minute and you'll come back with a new grip on life."

Trees and other growing things serve, in the Bible, to provide compelling images of fortitude, of abiding steadfastness. "I am the vine; you are the branches," said Jesus in order that we might see and understand what it means to abide, or to remain steadfast, in him (John 15:5). In Psalm 1, the righteous person is the rooted person—like a tree planted beside streams of water—while the wicked person is like chaff, blown away in the wind.

The selections in this chapter present us with a rich variety of natural images which can give us a new grip on life. Marlo Morgan observes that the kangaroo never steps backward. John Burroughs notes how just as obstacles in a brook can create a deep pool, his ideal brook; so, too, in a brave life. Images of the kneeling camel, the dancing deer, the enduring turtle, can fortify us, and even direct our prayer, as Elizabeth Barrett Browning prays, for the "patience taught by nature."

Assurances

I fortify myself with these:
The calm assurances of trees
That girdle with their sheltering boughs
The shelving rooftree of my house—
The friendly maple, and the pine
Whose pungence is an anodyne;
The ermined birch, the poplar slim,
The graceful ash, erect and trim.

By night my waking ear receives
The soothing gossip of their leaves;
By the warm light of day I see
Their elemental bravery.
They are my prop, they are my stay
Against all doubting and dismay;
They are my inspiration, these,
The stanch, the skyward-lifting trees!

CLINTON SCOLLARD

Born in Clinton, New York, where his father was a physician, Clinton Scollard (1860–1932) loved the outdoors and was active in sports. He attended the local Hamilton College, then pursued graduate studies at Harvard. At this time, his poems began appearing widely in such magazines as *Harper's* and *The Atlantic Monthly*. In 1888, Clinton Scollard returned to Hamilton College as a professor of English, where he was quite popular for his love of literature and the personal attention he gave to his students. He was the author of more than forty volumes of poetry, fiction and essays.

A Lesson from the Kangaroo

They spoke of the kangaroo—the silent, usually gentle creature that grows from two to seven feet tall and is found in earth colors of soft silver-gray to copper red. At birth the red kangaroo is the size and weight of one kidney bean, yet at maturity it stands seven feet tall. They think Mutants make too much of skin colors and body shapes. The main lesson taken from the kangaroo is that it does not step backward. It is not possible for it. It always goes forward, even when going around in circles! Its long tail is like the trunk of a tree and bears its weight. Many people choose the kangaroo as their totem because they feel a real kinship and recognize the necessity of learning balance in their personality. I liked the idea of looking back over my life and considering, even when it appeared I had made mistakes or poor choices; on some level of my being, it was the best I could do at the time. In the long run it was going to prove to be a step forward.

MARLO MORGAN

Marlo Morgan learned many lessons about living from her travels as an American woman among the nomadic Aboriginals (the "real people") of the Australian Outback. (There, outsiders are the "mutants"). Any animal to which one feels a particular kinship can serve as a "totem" or emblem of one's life.

Trees and Folks

"Last time I was up this way that tree was kind of drooping and discouraged. Grown trees act that way sometimes, same's folks; then they'll put right to it and strike their roots off into new ground and start all over again with real good courage. Ash-trees is very likely to have poor spells; they ain't got the resolution of other trees."

I listened hopefully for more; it was this peculiar wisdom that made one value Mrs. Todd's pleasant company.

"There's sometimes a good hearty tree growin' right out of the bare rock, out o' some crack that just holds the roots"; she went on to say, "right on the pitch o' one o' them bare stony hills where you can't seem to see a wheel-barrowful o'good earth in a place, but that tree'll keep a green top in the driest summer. You lay your ear down to the ground an' you'll hear a little stream runnin'. Every such tree has got its own livin' spring; there's folk made to match 'em."

SARAH ORNE JEWETT

In 1896, Sarah Orne Jewett (1849–1909) wrote *The Country of the Pointed Firs,* a quiet masterpiece, set on the coast of Maine, about several old women whose lives were tenaciously rooted in that rugged landscape. The book fell out of print until the mid-twentieth century, and has now become a literary classic. It evokes a sense of kinship with the earth and reclaims seemingly forgotten human values: sympathy, friendship, wisdom, and understanding. Throughout, its "pointed firs" gently but persistently point to a transcendent presence in the natural world.

Growth of Pines

Growing seems to be a common trait among living things.
But I wonder if anyone's ever done it better than an old pine.

If you're a pine, growth seems to have a lot to do with
making the best of where you get started. Sometimes that's
just a bare-bones, blustery, rocky outcrop of a place, inhospitable, with little soil or shelter, nurturing or encouragement. It
may take a long time, but you somehow come to grips with it—
this starting place. You reach and reach, stretching needy roots over
naked granite, through tiny cracks, down into crevices. Until you
finally find the footholds, the stability and sustenance you need. Then, someday,
somehow, you transcend…growing up, while at the same time growing down, and
growing out. Growing through all kinds of disasters. Growing through them.

And that's all there is to it, it seems. Grow. Down. Out. Up. Don't stop. Just
grow.

Simple enough. But maybe it's the hardest, most important thing in the world.
Maybe everything depends on it. Maybe the whole world depends on it.

Douglas Wood

As a young teacher in Minnesota, Douglas Wood first encountered the writings of Sigurd
F. Olson, and his life was changed. Wood has also worked as a wilderness guide and musi-
cian. His children's book, *Old Turtle,* has won numerous awards. He is also the author of
Paddle Whispers (1993) and *Minnesota, Naturally* (1995).

Patience Taught by Nature

'O dreary life,' we cry, 'O dreary life!'
And still the generations of the birds
Sing through our sighing, and the flocks and herds
Serenely live while we are keeping strife
With Heaven's true purpose in us, as a knife
Against which we may struggle! Ocean girds
    Unslackened the dry land, savannah-swards
    Unweary sweep, hills watch unworn, and rife
    Meek leaves drop yearly from the forest-trees
    To show, above, the unwasted stars that pass
In their old glory: O thou God of old,
Grant me some smaller grace than comes to these!
    But so much patience as a blade of grass
        Grows by, contented through the heat and cold.

ELIZABETH BARRETT BROWNING

Elizabeth Barrett Browning (1806–61) was born near Durham, England. Throughout her life, she suffered a series of illnesses and losses. The publication of her collection of poems in 1844, which included this sonnet, led to a secret correspondence with another poet, Robert Browning, whom she married two years later at the age of 40. Many still know her famous sonnet, "How Do I Love Thee? Let Me Count the Ways."

Lessons from Running Brooks

The angler learns that it is generally some obstacle or hindrance that makes a deep place in the creek, as in a brave life; and his ideal brook is one that lies in deep, well-defined banks, yet makes many a shift from right to left, meets with many rebuffs and adventures, hurled back upon itself by rocks, waylaid by snags and trees, tripped up by precipices, but sooner or later reposing under meadow banks, deepening and eddying beneath bridges, or prosperous and strong in some level stretch of cultivated lands with great elms shading it here and there.

❧

The lesson in running brooks is that motion is a great purifier and health-producer. When the brook ceases to run, it soon stagnates. It keeps in touch with the great vital currents when it is in motion, and unites with other brooks to help make the river. In motion it soon leaves all mud and sediment behind. Do not proper work and the exercise of will power have the same effect upon our lives?

JOHN BURROUGHS

Literary naturalist John Burroughs (1837–1921), who is credited with developing the nature essay as a vibrant literary form, helped to bring an end to the trend of anthropomorphism among the Victorian era of nature writers. His descriptions of nature were clear, direct, and insightful. He was the author of more than twenty-five volumes, including *Time and Change* and *Locusts and Wild Honey,* in which these selections appear.

The Snail's Lesson

Deep into the midst of a great, dark, wood,
Where shades are ever staying,
I found a snail, at the root of an oak,
One day, as I was maying;
And I said, "Oh stupid snail, so weak,
What moral high, canst thy poor life teach?"

And methought, the snail answered thus from his shell,
"Oh maid! List to my teaching;
Cautiously taking full time as I do,
I'm spared of over-reaching;
If you too, like me would take life more slow,
You truly would be benefited, I know."

"And I leave a silver trace in the rear,
So that, when false friends cavil,
I may turn, for reference, back to my path,
And prove how straight I travel;
Oh! If you'd leave in your rear, a fair trace,
'Twould serve you quite fitly the future to face."

"I lug on my back, wherever I go,
This house, my life protecting;
Oh maid! Though it slackens my speed the while,
I'm safe when foes are besetting;
And it would be safer if you were enrobed,
In the strong defense of Jesus, your Lord."

Priscilla Jane Thompson

African American poet Pricilla Jane Thompson was born in 1882 in Rossmoyne, Ohio. In 1900, she published her first book of poetry, *Ethiope Lays,* which included this lesson. "I have endeavored," she wrote in her preface to that book, "to picture the real side of my race bringing in the foreground, their patience, fortitude, and forbearance. . . ."

Consider the Turtle

Consider the turtle. . . . Perchance you have worried, despaired of the world, meditated the end of life, and all things seemed rushing to destruction; but nature has steadily and serenely advanced with the turtle's pace. The young turtle spends its infancy within its shell. It gets experience and learns the way of the world through that wall. While it rests warily on the edge of its hole, rash schemes are undertaken by men and fail. Has not the tortoise also learned the true value of time? You go to India and back, and the turtle eggs in your field are still unhatched. French empires rise or fall, but the turtle is developed only so fast. What's a summer? Time for a turtle's egg to hatch. So is the turtle developed, fitted to endure, for he outlives twenty French dynasties. One turtle knows several Napoleons. They have seen no berries, had no cares, yet has not the great world existed for them as much as for you?

HENRY DAVID THOREAU

From the time of Aesop's fables, the turtle has been regarded as a natural symbol of perseverance. "Behold the turtle," quipped James B. Conant. "He makes progress only when he sticks his neck out." Henry David Thoreau (1817–62) was 39 when he wrote this reflection on the turtle in his journal (August 28, 1856).

Dance of the Deer

One day I took a walk near my island home. Across the road a rufous doe grazed in the meadow with her new fawn—a picture of docility. A large yellow dog sauntered down the road toward me. He was bulky and intimidating, even from a distance. He stopped at the edge of the road to watch the doe and her fawn in the meadow. The fawn went on munching grass. The doe glanced up at the big dog, and then continued grazing. As I neared the dog, the fawn moved a few feet away from its mother. The dog sized up the scene very carefully. The moment he saw a beeline between himself and the fawn, he shot toward it at lightning speed. I shouted, as if that would stop him, but my voice mattered little. For a brief second it looked as if the fawn would be done for, and then I saw the rufous doe behave as I'd never seen before. She raised up tall and filled her chest with air, magnifying her size. She swiftly positioned herself between the dog and her fawn. Then she directly faced the dog. I feared he'd go for her throat and take her down, but no. Instead he hesitated before her. Then she advanced toward him stomping like a flamenco dancer. Her sharp black hooves pummeled the earth. It was quite impressive. At this the dog retreated. I hoped that would be the end of it. He left them in the meadow and returned to the road. I shooed him and commanded, "Go home!" But he was still intrigued.

He stayed there at the road's edge, eyeing the deer, waiting for another opening. The doe seemed as casual as could be. She grazed without looking up. She allowed the fawn to wander. She could surely hear me shooing the dog, but she seemed to pay us no mind. At last the dog saw his chance. He darted across the field toward the fawn. The fawn seemed oblivious, but the doe moved more fleetly than before. In an instant she was protectively positioned to guard her fawn. She reared up to show the dog her height. Then she advanced toward him, hammering her hooves in his face, mincing the grass at her feet. He moved backward a few steps. She kept pounding. Her hooves could easily have gouged out his eye or punctured his chest. But she seemed to want to demonstrate the threat of it without actually doing the damage. He turned tail and ran several feet as he had done before. But this time she kept coming, tearing up the sod beneath her hooves as she advanced. The dog ran to the road, then turned around to watch her. She held her ground at the edge of the road. He lowered his head to threaten another advance, and she puffed up and thumped the earth again as if to say, "Just try it, Buster." It was daunting, this dance of hers. The dog wanted no more of it and skulked away down the road.

Since then I've concluded the rufous doe is a superb model for any woman. Her gentle calm is appropriate for nearly every situation, except the rare occasions when sali-vating jaws threaten. Then it's necessary to have a set of sharp hooves up one's sleeve and the resolve to keep stomping until the predator retreats. When people praise doe-eyed gentleness, I don't argue, but I'll never forget she can be every bit as fierce as she is soft.

Since then, when life brings me face-to-face with a predator, my knees still knock and my legs tremble. But now I know this is more than a reflex, more than just fear. It's the dance of the deer stirring inside—it's my hooves warming up—preparing to stomp.

ERICA HELM MEADE

Erica Helm Meade is a counselor who uses stories in her practice of therapy. She is the author of *Telling It by Heart: Women and the Healing Power of Story* (1995), and *The Moon in the Well: Using Wisdom Tales to Transform Your Life, Family, and Community* (2000).

The Kneeling Camel

The camel at the close of day
Kneels down upon the sandy plain
To have his burden lifted off
And rest again.

My soul, thou too shouldst to thy knees
When daylight draweth to a close,
And let thy Master lift thy load,
And grant repose.

Else how canst thou tomorrow meet,
With all tomorrow's work to do,
If thou thy burden all the night
Dost carry through?

The camel kneels at break of day
To have his guide replace his load,
Then rises up anew to take
The desert road.

So thou shouldst kneel at morning dawn
That God may give thy daily care,
Assured that He no load too great
Will make thee bear.

ANNA TEMPLE WHITNEY

Only two species of camel exist today: the dromedary, or Arabian camel, which has one hump, and the mecheri, or Bactrian camel, which has two humps. In addition to the cushion-like pads on its feet, the camel also has tough pads on its legs for kneeling. When a camel kneels, it bends its front legs first, then its hind legs. It can both kneel and rise with a load of some 300 or 400 pounds, though it may groan or bawl as it rises with a heavy load.

I Think I Could Turn and Live with Animals

I think I could turn and live with animals, they are so placid
   and self-contain'd,
I stand and look at them long and long.

They do not sweat and whine about their condition,
They do not lie awake in the dark and weep for their sins,
They do not make me sick discussing their duty to God,
Not one is dissatisfied, not one is demented with the mania of owning things,
Not one kneels to another, nor to his kind that lived thousands of years ago,
Not one is respectable or unhappy over the whole earth.

So they show their relations to me and I accept them,
They bring me tokens of myself, they evince them plainly in their possession.

WALT WHITMAN

Walt Whitman (1819–92) was born on Long Island and worked as a journalist in Brooklyn. During the Civil War, he served as a hospital wound-dresser. Eventually he settled in Camden, New Jersey. Through all these years, Whitman worked continuously on his poetic masterpiece, *Leaves of Grass,* a book which sought to celebrate the vitality of American life in all its forms. Although his work was not always understood in his lifetime, Whitman is now regarded as one of America's greatest poets.

December Stillness

December stillness, teach me through your trees
That loom along the west, one with the land,
The veiled evangel of your mysteries.
While nightfall, sad and spacious, on the down
Deepens, and dusk imbues me, where I stand,
With grave diminishings of green and brown,
Speak, roofless Nature, your instinctive words;
And let me learn your secret from the sky,
Following a flock of steadfast, journeying birds
In lone remote migration beating by.
December stillness, crossed by twilight roads,
Teach me to travel far and bear my loads.

SIEGFRIED SASSOON

During World War I, Siegfried Sassoon (1886–1967) served as a captain in the British Army, receiving the Military Cross. He was best known in England for his intense, graphic poems of the war and its horrors. Born into a wealthy Jewish family, Sassoon converted to Catholicism in 1957, the same year he received the Queen's Medal for Poetry. Much of Sassoon's later poetry was distinctly spiritual in its themes.

Consider the Sea

Consider the subtleness of the sea; how its most dreaded creatures glide under water, unapparent for the most part, and treacherously hidden beneath the loveliest tints of azure. Consider also the devilish brilliance and beauty of many of its most remorseless tribes, as the dainty embellished shape of many species of sharks. Consider, once more, the universal cannibalism of the sea; all whose creatures prey upon each other, carrying on eternal war since the world began.

Consider all this; and then turn to this green, gentle, and most docile earth; consider them both, the sea and the land; and do you not find a strange analogy to something in yourself? For as this appalling ocean surrounds the verdant land, so in the soul of man there lies one insular Tahiti, full of peace and joy, but encompassed by all the horrors of the half known life. God keep thee! Push not off from that isle, thou canst never return!

HERMAN MELVILLE

Herman Melville (1819–91) was a sailor turned writer who composed several popular seagoing narratives. But when he wrote his masterpiece, *Moby Dick,* in 1851, it was virtually ignored. Not until the mid-twentieth century was it really discovered, and is now generally regarded as one of the most theologically searching novels America has produced. This selection from *Moby Dick* invites the reader to consider the contrasts between the sea and a tropical island, and to contemplate them both as aspects of one's spiritual geography, or inner landscape.

Practicing the Virtue of Fortitude

1. Identify one area in your life in which you need fortitude. Think of this area as a place in which you are going to start growing. Visualize the terrain. Is it a blustery, stony, outcrop of a place, such as that Sarah Orne Jewett or Douglas Wood describes? In your imagination begin to come to grips with this imagined place.

2. Follow Clinton Scollard's example. At the top of a sheet of paper, write, "I fortify myself with these." Then, make your own list of objects from nature that represent your sense of endurance or strength or courage or patience.

3. Consider some of the various trees in the Bible, and what they represent: the sycamore, the fig, the cedar. Then, consider the trees around you. What do they signify to you? Choose one tree, and imagine yourself as that tree.

4. As you kneel to pray, at the close of the day and at the break of day, imagine your burden as the camel's load. (See Anna Temple Whitney's poem.) Imagine it being lifted off for sleep, and resume it in the morning with God's strength. (See also Matthew 11:28-30.)

5. Ponder the "Lessons of Running Brooks." Consider, also, the ways in which running water has shaped the earth (e.g., the formation of the Mississippi Delta, the carving of the Grand Canyon). Or consult a concordance to the Bible, and make a list of all the many references to rivers and streams (e.g., Psalm 1:3 and 43:1; Isaiah 43:19; John 7:30). Fortify yourself with these lessons.

6. Herman Melville urges us to consider the sea and the land, and to "find a strange analogy to something in yourself." Identify one island in your life that you associate with peace and joy and solace. Imagine everything else in your life as part of the savage sea that surrounds that ocean. Visualize yourself living an islanded life, and "push not off from that isle."

7. Erica Helm Meade concludes that the doe "is a superb model for any woman." Margo Morgan admires the kangaroo because it cannot go backwards, but must always move forwards. Consider particular animals or plants you admire, and choose one as your "totem," a model you can keep in mind when life brings you face-to-face with obstacles or predators. You may even want to consider some of the many suggestions from the Bible (e.g., you are the branches; you are like sheep, etc.).

Temperance

Nature's Instruction
for Living with Limits

TEMPERANCE, TO TWENTY-FIRST CENTURY EARS, seems like such an antique word. It's probably the least appealing of the virtues, implying to many a dreary restriction of life's sensual pleasures. Let's face it: self-denial simply does not sell.

The ancients regarded temperance as a necessary balance between extremes. Cicero said, "Temperance is the moderating of one's desires in obedience to reason." Benjamin Franklin ranked it first in his famous list of thirteen virtues, explaining: "Temperance first, as it tends to procure that coolness and clearness of head. . . ."

Today, in American culture, the idea of moderating one's desires seems passé. We simply don't like limits. We have an expansive drive, shaped by the frontier myth of boundless opportunities and limitless resources. We hate to be confined, whether by city limits or credit limits or speed limits. Growth, for us, means more: more market share, more space, more stuff. Rather than moderate our desires, we fan them into needs. The luxuries of one generation become the necessities of the next.

Our temptations to excess are not merely material. We've grown accustomed to displays of unrestrained anger, uncontrolled pride, and unchecked power. The word *extreme* is a favorite superlative in our social vocabulary, applied without irony to sports and entertainment and a love of adventure.

Nature provides a startling antidote to the excesses of our culture. Nature teaches we are finite beings. Nature reminds us that we all deteriorate and die, and that others will replace us. Nature's economy is not one of boundless expansion, but a complex web of interdependencies. Living things learn to live within nature's limits.

In the natural world, when a growing population of any species overshoots its carrying capacity—that is, when it becomes larger than its habitat can support—it dies back precipitously. Sometimes it takes many generations to recover; sometimes it may never completely recover. Ecologists, like Garrett Hardin, warn us that humans, too, must begin grappling with nature's limits. We have been living as if resources are without limit. "Most ecological problems," Hardin writes in his book *Living Within Limits,* "reduce to the single problem of balancing supply and demand."

Temperance is a virtue that enables us to live our lives in balance. It is not about arbitrary rules nor about some austere denial. Rather, the restraints of temperance are really about self-preservation. There's a reason why temperance has been so often applied to the physical appetites; it's simply because the sexual drives and the drives for food and drink are nature's forces of survival. Without them, we would not continue. But unchecked, these drives can also become destructive. Temperance, then, is nature's virtue. Temperance deals with the integrity and preservation of one's self. Temperance, as Thomas Aquinas once defined it, is "a disposition of the soul" that keeps the passions within limits *(Summa Theologica).*

How does one acquire this disposition of the soul? The writers in this chapter turn to nature and find there inspiring models of life in balance. The great ornithologist, Roger Tory Peterson, explains how birds, living freely within limits, gave him a key to "unlock eternal things." Margot Lasher writes of the manatee that lives at the center of extremes. A whale teaches Herman Melville how to "live in this world without being of it." Throughout, Nature's instruction is more positive than negative; it's not so much about self-denial as it is about the joy and contentment in a life well-balanced. "O to be self-balanced for contingencies," wrote Walt Whitman; "To confront night, storms, hunger, ridicule, accidents, rebuffs, as the trees and animals do."

A "serenity of spirit" *(quies animi)* is another definition that Thomas Aquinas gave to temperance. Serenity is essentially a balancing act; it takes practice. Ralph Waldo Emerson, in his famous essay on "Self-Reliance," explained this sort of challenge succinctly: "It is easy in the world to live after the world's opinion; it is easy in solitude to live after our own; but the great man is he who in the midst of the crowd keeps with perfect sweetness the independence of solitude." To live a solitary life amid the crowd, or to live freely and independently within social constraints, is indeed challenging. But the rewards are even greater.

The selections in this chapter provide some provocative lessons from nature's balancing acts. Nature shows us freedom in restraint, life in the presence of death, warmth amid cold, abundance through scarcity. What we learn through these examples is that a temperate life is not a "reduced" life—as if that would be any virtue—but an enhanced life. To limit one's life so that one may gain a greater seems something of a paradox. Yet Jesus reminds us that to save our life we must lose it.

As Birds, Living with Limits

A bird can fly where it wants to when it wants to. I am sure that is what appealed to me when I was in school.

Regimentation and restriction rubbed me the wrong way; and the boys in my neighborhood were either younger or older, so I had to dream up my own fun. Birds seemed wonderful things. There were times when I wished that I could fly as they did and leave everything. . . .

As I learned more about birds I found they are not quite the gloriously unrestrained things I had imagined them to be. They are bound by all sorts of natural laws. They go north and south almost by the calendar. They seem to follow certain flyways and routes between their summer and winter homes. A robin that lives in Connecticut this year will not think of going to Wisconsin next year. . . . A night heron, newly arrived in the rookery, goes through a step-by-step ritual of song and dance. Leave out any one of the steps, and the sequence is disrupted—the reproductive cycle does not carry through. . . .

I learned, too, that most birds have "territory." The males hold down a plot of ground for their own—it maybe an acre or it may be five. They are property owners just as we are—and song, instead of being only a joyous outburst, is a functional expression—a proclamation of ownership, an invitation to a female, a threat to another male. . . .

Birds then, are almost as earth-bound as we are. They have freedom and mobility only within prescribed limits. . . .

Reluctant at first to accept the strait jacket of a world which I did not comprehend, I finally, with the help of my hobby, made some sort of peace with society. The birds, which started as an escape from the unreal, bridged the gap to reality and became a key whereby I might unlock eternal things.

ROGER TORY PETERSON

Roger Tory Peterson (1908–96) has been called "a modern John Jay Audubon" for his artistry of birds. His first book, *A Field Guide to the Birds,* published in 1934, sold millions of copies. In time he became editor of the famous series of Peterson Field Guides to nature. In 1950 he received the John Burroughs Medal for *Birds Over America* from which this selection is taken.

The Motion of the Manatee

Of all the animals I have known, I felt the deepest peacefulness from the manatees. They float in perfect synchrony with their world.

Every creature has a rhythm of motion in relation to the water, air, or land. Ground creatures move with little resistance from the air, except in a strong wind, and a lot of resistance from the ground. The air is so yielding around us, it touches us without our awareness. The ground is hard and full of resistance which we need to survive. We depend on the ground to be there, holding us in place. Underwater, or too high in space, we cannot breathe.

Water is both ground and air for its creatures, with powerful resistances of its own. Water is the solidity that keeps its inhabitants stable, and the permeability that lets them breathe. The water is always in motion—streams, currents, eddies, tides. A creature who lives in water is also in motion, with it or against it.

The rhythms of small reef fish and sea cucumbers create two extremes of underwater motion. A small fish darts around in the water, moving in short spurts from one point to another, then resting. During the rest it gathers the energy to spurt out again, breaking through the water. In the resting phase the fish floats with the current, but in the darting phase it outspeeds the water—spurt-rest; spurt-rest—creating a separate rhythm from its surroundings.

At the other extreme is the sea cucumber, who is connected to the rocks, physically and rhythmically. A sea cucumber looks like a rock under the water, dark gray covered with pale white algae. It moves incredibly slowly, clinging tightly to its anchoring solidity. The water washes over it, bathes, it, giving it breath. But it, too, has a separate rhythm from the water; its motion is closer to the stillness of a rock.

The manatee moves at the center of these extremes, at one with the rhythm of the water. The manatee floats inside the water. It is not the same floating as a leaf on top of the water, riding the waves; nor is it the same as that of the sea moss attached to the rocks at the bottom of the water, swaying with the current. When you watch the leaf and the sea moss you feel the power of the water and the yielding of leaf and plant. When you watch the manatee, you feel a perfect harmony between the motion of the water and the body of this large, round creature. You feel in the presence of inner peace.

MARGOT LASHER

Margot Lasher is a clinical psychologist and author.

Two Sides of a River

All rivers, small or large, agree in one character; they like to lean a little on one side; they cannot bear to have their channels deepest in the middle, but will always, if they can, have one bank to sun themselves upon, and another to get cool under; one shingly shore to play over, where they may be shallow, and foolish, and child-like; and another steep shore, under which they can pause and purify themselves, and get their strength of waves fully together for due occasions. Rivers in this way are just like wise men, who keep one side of their life for play, and another for work; and can be brilliant, and chattering, and transparent when they are at ease, and yet take deep counsel on the other side when they set themselves to the main purpose. And rivers are just in this way divided, also, like wicked and good men; the good rivers have serviceable deep places all along their banks that ships can sail in, but the wicked rivers go scoopingly, irregularly, under their banks until they get full of strangling eddies, which no boat can row over without being twisted against the rocks, and pools like wells which no one can get out of but the water-kelpie that lives at the bottom; but, wicked or good, the rivers all agree in having two sides.

JOHN RUSKIN

John Ruskin (1819–1900) graduated from Oxford University in 1842 and, against the wishes of his protective parents, became a prominent and prolific art critic. Among his major works was his five-volume *Modern Painters*. Ruskin lectured widely and was eventually appointed to a professorship at Oxford. But he also maintained a heart for social reform, which sometimes, in his privileged position, created great inner conflict. Today, Ruskin is still regarded as one of the finest prose stylists of the Victorian Age.

Living with Scarcity

The immensity of land and sky in the western Dakotas allows for few trees, and I love the way that treelessness reveals the contours of the land, the way that each tree that remains seems a message-bearer. I love what trees signify in the open country. The Audubon field book describes the bur oak as "a pioneer tree, invading the prairie grassland," and I try to listen to what these "volunteers" have to say about persistence, the strength of water, seeds , and roots, the awesome whimsy of birds scattering seed in their excrement, casting not only oak but small groves of Russian olive in their wake. Cottonwoods need more water; their presence signifies ground water, or the meanderings of a creek. Sometimes, in the distance, you glimpse what looks like a stand of scrub brush or chokecherry bushes. But if you turn off the asphalt two-lane highway onto a gravel road, you find that what you've seen is the tops of tall cottonwoods standing in glory along a creek bottom, accompanied by willows.

❧

The wisdom of the few, struggling trees on the Plains, and the vast spaces around them, are a continual reminder that my life is cluttered by comparison. At home, an abundance of books and papers overlays the heavy furniture I inherited from my grandparents. A perfectly simple room, with one perfect object to meditate on, remains a dream until I step outside, onto the Plains. A tree. A butte. The sunrise. It always makes me wonder: What is enough? Are there enough trees here? As always, it seems that the more I can distinguish between my true needs and my wants, the more I am shocked to realize how little *is* enough.

KATHLEEN NORRIS

More than twenty years ago, Kathleen Norris moved from New York to Lemmon, South Dakota, to rescue the estate of her grandparents. There she rediscovered her Protestant inheritance, a process she describes in her best-selling memoir, *Dakota: A Spiritual Geography* (1994). Norris describes herself as a Christian who settles neither for "the easy answers of fundamentalism" nor for the "over intellectualized banalities of conventional liberalized faith." Her recent books include *The Cloister Walk* (1996) and *Amazing Grace: A Vocabulary of Faith* (1998).

Under the Pressures of the Deep

At first thought it seems a paradox that creatures of such great fragility as the glass sponge and the jellyfish can live under the conditions of immense pressure that prevail in deep water. . . . For creatures at home in the deep sea, however, the saving fact is that the pressure inside their tissues is the same as that without, and, as long as this balance is preserved, they are no more inconvenienced by a pressure of a ton or so than we are by ordinary atmospheric pressure. And most abyssal creatures, it must be remembered, live out their whole lives in a comparatively restricted zone, and are never required to adjust themselves to extreme changes of pressure.

But of course there are exceptions, and the real miracle of sea life in relation to great pressure is not the animal that lives its whole life on the bottom, bearing a pressure of perhaps five or six tons, but those that regularly move up and down through hundreds or thousands of feet of vertical change. The small shrimps and other planktonic creatures that descend into deep water during the day are examples. Fish that possess air bladders, on the other hand, are vitally affected by abrupt changes of pressure, as anyone knows who has seen a trawler's net raised from a hundred fathoms. Apart from the accident of being captured in a net and hauled up through waters of rapidly diminishing pressures, fish may sometimes wander out of the zone to which they are adjusted and find themselves unable to return. Perhaps in their pursuit of food they roam upward to the ceiling of the zone that is theirs, and beyond whose invisible boundary they may not stray without meeting alien and inhospitable conditions. Moving from layer to layer of drifting plankton as they feed, they may pass beyond the boundary. In the lessened pressure of these upper waters the gas enclosed within the air bladder expands. The fish becomes lighter and more buoyant. Perhaps he tries to fight his way down again, opposing the upward lift with all the power of his muscles. If he does not succeed, he 'falls' to the surface, injured and dying, for the abrupt release of pressure from without causes distention and rupture of the tissues.

Rachel Carson

Rachel Carson (1907–64) was a biologist with the U.S. Fish and Wildlife Service when, in 1951, she became famous for her best-selling book, *The Sea Around Us.* Two years before her death from cancer, she published *Silent Spring,* which awakened the world to the dangers of pesticides and led to the banning of DDT in the United States.

Timelessness

Our lives seem governed by speed, tension, and hurry. We move so fast and are caught so completely in a web of confusion there is seldom time to think. Our cities are veritable beehives dominated by the sounds of traffic and industry. Even at the top of the highest building, one is conscious of the hive's human busyness.

The change of season is often unobserved, the coming of winter, spring, summer, and autumn. Winter merely means an aggravation of traffic and transportation, spring the sloshiness of rain, summer dust and heat, fall the withering of transplanted flowers and the threat of cold. For one who has lived in the wilderness, it is impossible to adjust to this, and each time I come away from the city, I feel drained of silence and naturalness.

During a trip into the wilds, it often takes men a week or more to forget the frenetic lives they have led, but inevitably the feeling of timelessness does come, often without warning. On a trip long ago, I remember the first impact of a rising full moon. We were in the open on a great stretch of water, with islands in the far distance. The sky gradually brightened and an orange slice of moon appeared; we watched as the great sight unfolded before us. At that moment, the city men in the party caught a hint of its meaning. They were entranced as the moon became clear: pulsating as though alive, it rose slowly above the serrated spruces of the far shore. Then, as it almost reluctantly paled, we took to our paddles again. We searched and searched and found a long point from which we could see both sunset and moonrise at the same time. The calling of the loons meant more after that, and as the dusk settled all were aware of something new in their lives.

I know now as men accept the time clock of the wilderness, their lives become entirely different. It is one of the great compensations of primitive experience, and when one finally reaches the point where days are governed by daylight and dark, rather than by schedules, where one eats if hungry and sleeps when tired, and becomes completely immersed in the ancient rhythms, then one begins to live.

SIGURD F. OLSON

Sigurd F. Olson (1899–1982) was an educator, conservationist, and writer who believed that wilderness preservation is "a spiritual necessity, an antidote to the high pressure of modern life." His first book, *The Singing Wilderness,* published when he was 57, became a best-seller, and many other books followed.

Autumn Psalm of Contentment

O sacred season of Autumn, be my teacher,
    for I wish to learn the virtue of contentment.
As I gaze upon your full-colored beauty,
    I sense all about you
    an at-homeness with your amber riches.

You are the season of retirement,
    of full barns and harvested fields.
The cycle of growth has ceased,
    and the busy work of giving life
    is now completed.
I sense in you no regrets:
    you've lived a full life.

I live in a society that is ever-restless,
    always eager for more mountains to climb,
    seeking happiness through more and more possessions.
As a child of my culture,
    I am seldom truly at peace with what I have.
Teach me to take stock of what I have given and received,
    may I know that it's enough,
    that my striving can cease
    in the abundance of God's grace.
May I know the contentment
    that allows the totality of my energies
    to come to full flower.
May I know that like you I am rich beyond measure. . . .

EDWARD HAYS

Edward Hays is a Roman Catholic priest whose work on spirituality and prayer has appealed widely to people from various religious traditions. "If God is the single parent from whom all life has come," he says in his *Prayers for a Planetary Pilgrim,* "then it follows that we are a single family." Such recognition, he insists, means that "prayers for justice and peace for all who dwell on this planet must be an essential part of our practice."

Poem of Praise

Swift things are beautiful:
swallows and deer,
and lightning that falls
bright-veined and clear,
rivers and meteors,
wind in the wheat,
the strong-withered horse,
the runner's sure feet.

And slow things are beautiful:
the closing of day,
the pause of the wave
that curves downward to spray,
the ember that crumbles,
the opening flower,
and the ox that moves on
in the quiet of power.

ELIZABETH COATSWORTH

Elizabeth Coatsworth (1893–1986) is best known as the author of the 1931 Newberry Medal winner, *The Cat Who Went to Heaven,* and numerous other books. In 1929, she married author Henry Beston. The Bestons collaborated on several children's books, such as *The Tree That Ran Away* (1941).

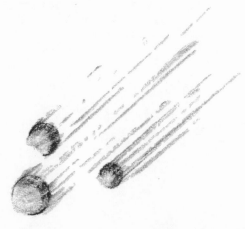

Fire and Water

When fire breaks loose and rages on its own account, it carries swift destruction in its course; but, when restricted within certain bounds, it warms our rooms and cooks our food, illuminates our towns and drives our locomotives. In the same way, water, when in flood, roots up trees, carries away houses, and sweeps the crops from the fields; but, when confined within its banks, drives the wheel and floats the barge and rejoices the eye, either by its placid flow or by the splendors of the cataract. So the very qualities that, when unregulated, waste and brutalize life may, when subjected to the control of temperance, be its fairest ornaments.

JAMES STALKER

James Stalker (1848–1927) was raised in Scotland, became a minister and, later, professor of church history at the United Free Church College in Aberdeen. In 1901, he published *The Seven Deadly Sins,* and the following year, *The Seven Cardinal Virtues,* in which this selection appears. "Temperance has to do with the enemies within," Dr. Stalker wrote; "with the lusts and passions that war against the soul."

Life and Death in the Forest

It is the peculiar nature of the forest, that life and death may ever be found within its bounds, in immediate presence of each other; both with ceaseless, noiseless, advances, aiming at the mastery; and if the influences of the first be most general, those of the last are the most striking. Spring, with all her wealth of life and joy, finds within the forest many a tree unconscious of her approach; a thousand young plants springing up about the fallen trunk, the shaggy roots, seek to soften the gloomy wreck with a semblance of the verdure it bore of old; but ere they have thrown their fresh and graceful wreaths over the moldering wood, half their own tribe wither and die with the year. We owe to this perpetual presence of death an impression, calm, solemn, almost religious in character, a chastening influence, beyond what we find in the open fields. But this subdued spirit is far from gloomy or oppressive, since it never fails to be relived by the cheerful animation of living beauty. Sweet flowers grow beside the fallen trees, among the shattered branches, the season through; and the freedom of the woods, the unchecked growth, the careless position of every tree, are favorable to a thousand wild beauties, and fantastic forms, opening to the mind a play of fancy which is in itself cheering and enlivening, like the bright sunbeams which checker with golden light the shadowy groves. That character of rich variety also, stamped on all the works of the creation, is developed in the forest in clear and noble forms; we are told that in the field we shall not find two blades of grass exactly alike, that in the garden we shall not gather two flowers precisely similar, but in those cases the lines are minute, and we do not seize the truth at once; in the woods, however, the same fact stands recorded in bolder lines; we cannot fail to mark this great variety of detail among the trees; we see it in their trunks, their branches, their foliage; in the rude knots, the gnarled roots; in the mosses and lichens which feed upon their bark; in their forms, their coloring, their shadows. And within all this luxuriance of varied beauty, there dwells a sweet quiet, a noble harmony, a calm repose, which we seek in vain elsewhere, in so full a measure.

SUSAN FENIMORE COOPER

Susan Fenimore Cooper (1813–94), daughter to the famous novelist James Fenimore Cooper spent most of her life in Cooperstown, New York. She served her community vigorously, establishing a shelter for poor people, as well as a hospital and an orphanage. This selection comes from her book, *Rural Hours* (1850).

Walking through a Prairie

There are several ways not to walk in the prairie, and one of them is with your eye on a far goal, because you then begin to believe you're not closing the distance any more than you would with a mirage. My woodland sense of scale and time didn't fit this country, and I started wondering whether I could reach the summit before dark. On the prairie, distance and the miles of air turn movement to stasis and openness to a wall, a thing as difficult to penetrate as dense forest. I was hiking in a chamber of absences where the near was the same as the far, and it seemed every time I raised a step the earth rotated under me so that my foot fell just where it had lifted from. Limits and markers make travel possible for people: circumscribe our lines of sight and we can really get somewhere. Before me lay the Kansas of popular conception from Coronado on—that place you have to get through, that purgatory of mileage.

But I kept walking, and, when I dropped into hollows and the mound disappeared, I focused on a rock or a tuft of grass to keep from convoluting my track. Hiking in woods allows a traveler to imagine comforting enclosures, one leading to the next, and the walker can possess those little encompassed spaces, but the prairie and plains permit no such possession. Whatever else prairie is—grass, sky, wind—it is most of all a paradigm of infinity, a clearing full of many things except boundaries, and its power comes from its apparent limitlessness; there is no such thing as a small prairie any more than there is a little ocean, and the consequence of both is this challenge: try to take yourself seriously out here, you bipedal plodder, you complacent cartoon.

WILLIAM LEAST HEAT MOON

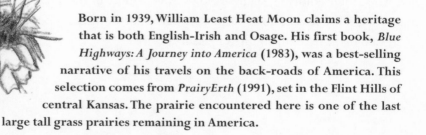

Born in 1939, William Least Heat Moon claims a heritage that is both English-Irish and Osage. His first book, *Blue Highways: A Journey into America* (1983), was a best-selling narrative of his travels on the back-roads of America. This selection comes from *PrairyErth* (1991), set in the Flint Hills of central Kansas. The prairie encountered here is one of the last large tall grass prairies remaining in America.

The Whale's Blanket

A word or two more concerning this matter of the skin or blubber of the whale. It has already been said, that it is stripped from him in long pieces, called blanket-pieces. Like most sea-terms, this one is very happy and significant. For the whale is indeed wrapt up in his blubber as in a real blanket or counterpane; or, still better, an Indian poncho slipt over his head, and skirting his extremity. It is by reason of this cosy blanketing of his body, that the whale is enabled to keep himself comfortable in all weathers, in all seas, times, and tides. What would become of a Greenland whale, say, in those shuddering, icy seas of the North, if unsupplied with his cosy surtout? True, other fish are found exceedingly brisk in those Hyperborean waters; but these, be it observed, are your cold-blooded, lungless fish, whose very bellies are refrigerators; creatures, that warm themselves under the lee of an iceberg, as a traveller in winter would bask before an inn fire; whereas, like man, the whale has lungs and warm blood. Freeze his blood, and he dies . . .

It does seem to me, that herein we see the rare virtue of a strong individual vitality, and the rare virtue of thick walls, and the rare virtue of interior spaciousness. Oh, man! admire and model thyself after the whale! Do thou, too, remain warm among ice. Do thou, too, live in this world without being of it. Be cool at the equator; keep thy blood fluid at the Pole. Like the great dome of St. Peter's, and like the great whale, retain, O man! in all seasons a temperature of thine own.

HERMAN MELVILLE

Although Herman Melville's masterpiece, *Moby Dick,* was ignored in his lifetime, it's depth and complexity are now widely recognized. Everything in the world of that novel is charged with meaning and significance. In this passage from *Moby Dick,* Melville (1819–91) finds meaning in the whale's blubber, or blanket, which was stripped away by the whalers. In Melville's imagination, this protective blanket represents some vital quality humans need to "live in this world without being of it."

Practicing the Virtue of Temperance

1. Make a list of specific things in your life that serve to limit your personal freedom. Choose one of those specific limitations, and consider the freedom that you enjoy within those limits. Consider, also, any advantages you may experience as a result of that limitation. Pray for the ability to see your limitations as being a natural definition to your life, and not as a restraining straitjacket.

2. Practice living with the independence of solitude in the midst of a crowd, as Emerson describes in the introduction to this chapter.

3. Consider the manatee as a model for living between extremes. Define the "extremes" of your life: Where is the hard, solid ground for you? Where is the lightness of air? Visualize moving, as the manatee moves, peacefully between these extremes. Imagine how you might float in perfect synchrony with your world.

4. Edward Hays finds autumn as his sacred season of contentment. Which of the seasons speaks of contentment for you? Try writing your own psalm to this season, listing the qualities of the season that you want to apply to your life.

5. To Herman Melville, the whale, with its thick blubber, illustrates "the rare virtue of a strong individual vitality, and the rare virtue of thick walls, and the rare virtue of interior spaciousness." These qualities enable the whale to live in its world without being of it. How might you model yourself after the whale?

6. After pondering the few straggling trees on the great plains, Kathleen Norris sees her life as cluttered. Take stock of your surroundings. What are your true needs and wants? What would it mean for you to choose the spare world over the abundant?

7. On paper, visualize your life like John Ruskin's river. Think of this river as having two sides. (What are they? What do the two sides represent for you?) Sketch the course of your life, including all the bends, oxbows and constrictions of your experience. Then, as you study this chart of your experience, draw in the channel. Your channel may hug one shore in some places, and the opposite shore in other places. But the channel is your freedom!

Justice

Nature's Instruction
for Living in Right
Relationships

WE HAVE NO PROBLEM EXPOSING AND DENOUNCING INJUSTICE. It's justice we find difficult to identify and to practice. People denounce injustice, Plato observed long ago, "fearing that they may be victims of it and not because they shrink from committing it."

Justice implies a responsibility to others. This is what distinguishes it from the other classical virtues. While prudence, temperance, and fortitude shape one's personal character, justice is directed toward others. Or, as Augustine put it, "Justice is the virtue that gives each his due."

Part of the difficulty we have with justice is simply accepting our own responsibility. Our litigious society makes it easy to adopt a victim mentality, blaming others, or blaming circumstances and conditions in order to justify one's behavior. We are not being encouraged to care for one another.

A larger problem with justice emerges when we begin thinking about what it is we actually owe to others. Individuals, one-on-one, may be guided by the fundamental respect of the Golden Rule: "Do unto others as you would have them do unto you." But in a pluralistic society, how do we render justice to all? What theory of justice enables us to decide what is owed to whom? On what basis do we distribute our nation's wealth? How do we provide adequate health care for all citizens? What is owed to the elderly? What responsibility do wealthy nations have to developing nations? How do we adequately compensate those who have been torn away from their homeland? How does a society establish a right relationship between the common good and the individual good? Such questions continue to provoke endless and sometimes bitter discussions.

Justice, as a principle, is an exercise of power that may be shaped, or mis-shaped, by our laws and agreements about what we consider right. But justice is also a virtue, a quality of seeking right relationships. For a Christian, justice must be animated by love, by genuine concern for the welfare of others.

Shakespeare dramatized this important distinction between justice as a principle and justice as a virtue in his problem play, *The Merchant of Venice*. A much-abused money lender, Shylock, has made an outrageous but legal contract with the merchant Antonio, and insists before the court that the contract be honored. He craves justice, both the justice of the law and the justice of retribution. Portia, the wise counselor, pleads with Shylock to show mercy, because:

It is an attribute to God himself;
And earthly power doth then show likest God's
When mercy seasons justice.

What we owe each other, she argues, is the treatment we expect from God. "Consider this," she urges:

> *That in the course of justice, none of us*
> *Should see salvation. We do pray for mercy,*
> *And that same prayer doth teach us all to render*
> *The deeds of mercy.*

A right relationship, then, is one which is characterized by this sort of equity: what we pray to receive, that we should also show to others.

Jesus, in response to the Mosaic concept of justice which asserted, "Eye for eye, and tooth for tooth," put forth a radical concept: "If someone strikes you on the right cheek, turn to him the other also" (Matthew 5:38-9). Many have found this commandment difficult to understand and even more difficult to practice. The famous biologist, Konrad Lorenz, received a new understanding of Jesus' words from a surprising source—a fight between two wolves. His account of that lesson is included in this chapter.

Can nature teach us justice? Perhaps not by direct example. Justice is a human quality; and nature, as another biologist put it, is concerned with equilibrium, not equality. But nature can instruct us in developing right relationships.

First, nature shows us that our lives are intricately connected with others, both natural and human. In our ignoring this fact, we have contributed to so much environmental injustice. We have acted as conquerors, not as citizens of a biotic community, said the great conservationist, Aldo Leopold, more than half a century ago. The environmental problems we are experiencing today stem directly from our not loving the earth, the water, the plants and animals. A "land ethic," Leopold argued, implies respect for fellow-members of the natural world and for ourselves as part of that community. "If we were really to think of ourselves as indispensable elements of nature," biologist Lewis Thomas observes, "it would mean making some quite fundamental changes in our attitudes toward each other." Barbara Kingsolver, Michael Tlanusta Garrett, Luther Standing Bear, Paul Gruchow and others in this chapter, encourage us to understand some of the implications for seeing ourselves as indispensable parts of nature, and of each other.

Second, nature instructs us in seeing individuals more justly. "We need another and a wiser and perhaps a more mystical concept of animals," observed Henry Beston in *The Outermost House,*. his reflective work on living alone on the beach of Cape Cod.

In a world older and more complete than ours they move finished and complete, gifted with extensions of the senses we have lost or never attained, living by voices we shall never hear. They are not brethren, they are not underlings; they are other nations, caught with ourselves in the net of life and time, fellow prisoners of the splendor and travail of the earth.

To treat living things justly, we must see them as they are, in their own identity. And so with humans. This is not to elevate plants and animals to a human level, nor to reduce humans to the animal. It is about seeing "the other" clearly and justly.

The selections that follow provide some lessons in seeing natural things on their own terms, in their own identity. "Each particular being, in its individuality, its concrete nature and entity," Thomas Merton explains, "gives glory to God by being precisely what He wants it to be here and now."

Simple Forms of Justice

Many animals observe the conditions of fair play, of "equity"—that is, justice in a larger sense than our human law. It is seen in one of its simplest forms at a bird bath. Several birds often sit on the edge, one by one taking turns at enjoying the water. A time approaching one minute usually is allowed each bird to throw the bright cleansing drops over his back and wings. If he takes longer the next bird will challenge him. The bather may bluster a bit but he always leaves, and the others wait patiently until all have a chance. Taking turns at some favored activity is seen constantly in the wilderness, and far down the biological scale.

And speaking of justice, the Finnish anthropologist E. A. Westermarck made an interesting observation: that an outraged animal does not strike out blindly, venting his anger on anyone happening to be near. He is "discriminating in his retribution," punishing only the offender and sometimes waiting for a considerable length of time for that opportunity.

The great English jurist Blackstone said that our property laws are based on the concepts of ownership shown by most animals. Even spiders respect the webs of other spiders unless their own have been destroyed, and among other species the separate members of a group are allowed to keep any desirable territories they have claimed, to have their homes, their nests or burrows inviolate. The stronger birds or animals would be able to rout them, but even in species which have developed hierarchies based on dominance or leadership, the "boss" recognizes the property rights of the weaker.

SALLY CARRIGHAR

Sally Carrighar (1898–1985) was well into middle age when she became a nature writer. She had spent years working at various office jobs, writing financial articles and advertising copy. A suggestion from a National Park Service naturalist prompted her to study wildlife in the Sequoia National Park, resulting in her first nature book, *One Day on Beetle Rock* (1944). Carrighar found a "healing" power in nature, and her books reached a popular audience. *Wild Heritage,* published in 1965, helped to define a new field of ethology—the science of animal behavior. Responding to critics who frequently faulted her work for its anthropomorphism, Carrighar insisted that "it is not anthropomorphic at all to say that our behavior is related to that of the animals. The point is not that the animals are like us but that we are like them."

Making Peace

When a male bird—a vireo, for example—sings his belligerent
song at another male vireo that approaches his neck of the woods,
he is singing about family. It's a little bit like grumbling over the
handsome delivery person who's getting too friendly with your
spouse; a lot like coming with a crowbar after an intruder at your
child's bedroom window in the night; and nothing at all like a no
trespassing sign. The vireo doesn't waste his breath on the
groundhogs gathering chestnuts under his nose, or the walnut
trees using the sunlight to make their food, the grubs churn-
ing leaves into soil, the browsing deer, or even other birds
that come to glean seeds that are useless to a vireo's children.
Worm-eating birds have no truck with seedeaters; small-seed eaters ignore big-
seed eaters. This is the marvelous construct of "niche," the very particular way an
organism uses its habitat, and it allows for an almost incomprehensible degree of
peaceful coexistence. Choose a cubic foot of earth, about anywhere that isn't
paved; look closely enough, and you'll find that thousands of different kinds of living things are sharing that place, each one merrily surviving on something its neighbors couldn't use for all the tea in China. I'm told that nine-tenths of human law is
about possession. But it seems to me we don't know the first thing about it.

BARBARA KINGSOLVER

Born in 1955, novelist Barbara Kingsolver holds a masters degree in biology and ecology,
and worked as a technical writer before the publication of her first novel, *The Bean Trees*
(1988). Since then, she has become a best-selling author, and her writing has been widely
admired for its inspiration and insight. Kingsolver's novels are especially known for her
portrayals of resilient women characters. Many of her works include vibrant descriptions
of nature, such as *High Tide in Tucson* (1995) in which this selection appears. Other recent
books include *The Poisonwood Bible* (1998) and *Prodigal Summer* (2000).

Kinship with All Creatures
of Earth, Sky, and Water

Kinship with all creatures of the earth, sky, and water was a real and active principle. For the animal and bird world there existed a brotherly feeling that kept the Lakota safe among them and so close did some of the Lakotas come to their feathered and furred friends that in true brotherhood they spoke a common tongue.

The animal had rights—the right of man's protection, the right to live, the right to multiply, the right to freedom, and the right to man's indebtedness—and in recognition of these rights the Lakota never enslaved the animal, and spared all life that was not needed for food and clothing.

This concept of life and its relations was humanizing and gave to the Lakota an abiding love. It filled his being with the joy and mystery of living; it gave him reverence for all life;
it made a place for all things in the scheme of
existence with equal importance to all. The Lakota could despise no creature, for all were of one blood, made by the same hand, and filled with the essence of the Great Mystery. In spirit the Lakota was humble and meek. 'Blessed are the meek: for they shall inherit the earth,' was true for the Lakota, and from the earth he inherited secrets long since forgotten. . . .

But the old Lakota was wise. He knew that man's heart, away from nature, becomes hard; he knew that lack of respect for growing, living things soon led to lack of respect for humans too.

LUTHER STANDING BEAR

Born on the Sioux Pine Reservation in the 1860s, Luther Standing Bear became a lifelong advocate for Native American rights and sought to preserve the wisdom and customs of his people. His first book, *My People, The Sioux*, was published in 1928. Before his death in 1939, Standing Bear lived and worked in Hollywood as an actor.

The Community Concept

All ethics so far evolved rest upon a single premise: that the individual is a member of a community of interdependent parts. His instincts prompt him to compete for his place in the community, but his ethics prompt him also to co-operate (perhaps in order that there may be a place to compete for).

The land ethic simply enlarges the boundaries of the community to include soils, waters, plants, and animals, or collectively: the land.

This sounds simple: do we not already sing our love for and obligation to the land of the free and the home of the brave? Yes, but just what and whom do we love? Certainly not the soil, which we are sending helter-skelter downriver. Certainly not the waters, which we assume have no function except to turn turbines, float barges, and carry off sewage. Certainly not the plants, of which we exterminate whole communities without batting an eye. Certainly not the animals, of which we have already extirpated many of the largest and most beautiful species. A land ethic of course cannot prevent the alteration, management, and use of these 'resources,' but it does affirm their right to continued existence, and, at least in spots, their continued existence in a natural state.

In short, a land ethic changes the role of Homo sapiens from conqueror of the land-community to plain member and citizen of it. It implies respect for his fellow-members, and also respect for the community as such.

ALDO LEOPOLD

Aldo Leopold (1886–1948) was a forester and naturalist for the U.S. Forest Service for nearly twenty years before his appointment to the University of Wisconsin. Leopold believed that ethics, rather than economics, should guide our relationship to the land. He summed up his famous "land ethic" this way: "A thing is right when it tends to preserve the integrity, stability, and beauty of the biotic community. It is wrong when it tends otherwise." Aldo Leopold is now regarded as one the foremost ecologists of the twentieth century. His book of meditations on nature, *A Sand County Almanac,* continues to be widely read.

The Rejected Tree

Hui-tse said to Chuang-tse, "I have a large tree which no carpenter can cut into lumber. Its branches and trunk are crooked and tough, covered with bumps and depressions. No builder would turn his head to look at it. Your teaching are the same—useless, without value. Therefore, no one pays attention to them.

"As you know," Chuang-tse replied, "a cat is very skilled at capturing its prey. Crouching low, it can leap in any direction, pursuing whatever it is after. But when its attention is focused on such things, it can be easily caught with a net. On the other hand, a huge yak is not easily caught or overcome. It stands like a stone, or a cloud in the sky. But for all its strength it cannot catch a mouse.

"You complain that your tree is not valuable as lumber. But you could make use of the shade it provides, rest under its sheltering branches, and stroll beneath it, admiring its character and appearance. Since it would not be endangered by an axe, what could threaten its existence? It is useless to you only because you want to make it into something else and do not use it in its proper way."

CHUANG TSU,
AS RETOLD BY BENJAMIN HOFF

This story was told by Chuang Tsu, around the fourth century B.C.E., and is retold by Benjamin Hoff in *The Tao of Pooh* (1982). In this book, and in his second book, *The Te of Piglet* (1992), Hoff borrows the characters from A. A. Milne's *Winnie the Pooh* and overlays them with Taoist philosophy.

On Turning the Other Cheek

An enormous old timber wolf and a rather weaker, obviously younger one are the opposing champions and they are moving in circles round each other, exhibiting admirable "footwork." At the same time, the bared fangs flash in such a rapid exchange of snaps that the eye can scarcely follow them. So far, nothing has really happened. The jaws of one wolf close on the gleaming white teeth of the other who is on the alert and wards off the attack. Only the lips have received one or two minor injuries. The younger wolf is gradually being forced backwards. It dawns upon us that the older one is purposely maneuvering him towards the fence. We wait with breathless anticipation what will happen when he "goes to the wall." Now he strikes the wire netting, stumbles … and the old one is upon him. And now the incredible happens, just the opposite of what you would expect. The furious whirling of the gray bodies has come to a sudden standstill. Shoulder to shoulder they stand, pressed against each other in a stiff and strained attitude, both heads now facing in the same direction. Both wolves are growling angrily, the elder in a deep bass, the younger in higher tones, suggestive of the fear that underlies his threat. But notice carefully the position of the two opponents; the older wolf has his muzzle close, very close against the neck of the younger, and the latter holds away his head, offering unprotected to his enemy the bend of his neck, the most vulnerable part of his whole body! Less than an inch from the tensed neck muscles, where the jugular vein lies immediately beneath the skin, gleam the fangs of his antagonist from beneath the wickedly retracted lips. Whereas, during the thick of the fight, both wolves were intent on keeping only their teeth, the one invulnerable part of the body, in opposition to each other, it now appears that the discomfited fighter proffers intentionally that part of his anatomy to which a bite must assuredly prove fatal. Appearances are notoriously deceptive, but in this case, surprisingly, they are not.

❧

Every second you expect violence and await with bated breath the moment when the winner's teeth will rip the jugular vein of the loser. But your fears are groundless, for it will not happen. In this particular situation, the victor will definitely not close on his less fortunate rival. You can see that he would like to, but he just cannot! A dog or wolf that offers its neck to its adversary in this way will never be bitten seriously. The other growls and grumbles, snaps with his teeth in the empty air and even carries out, without delivering so much as a bit, the movement of shaking something to death in the empty air. However, this strange inhibition from biting persists only so long as the defeated dog or wolf maintains his attitude of humility. Since the fight is stopped so suddenly by this action, the victor frequently finds himself straddling his vanquished foe in anything but a comfortable position. So to remain, with his muzzle applied to the neck of the "underdog" soon becomes tedious for the champion, and, seeing that he cannot bite anyway, he soon withdraws. Upon this, the underdog may hastily attempt to put distance between himself and his superior. But he is not usually successful in this, for, as soon as he abandons his rigid attitude of submission, the other again falls upon him like a thunderbolt and the victim must again freeze into his former posture.

❧

The worker in comparative ethology does well to be very careful in applying moral criteria to animal behavior. But here, I must myself own to harboring sentimental feelings: I think it a truly magnificent thing that one wolf finds himself unable to bite the proffered neck of the other, but still more so that the other relies upon him for this amazing restraint. Mankind can learn a lesson from this, from the animal that Dante calls *"la bestia senza pace."* I at least have extracted from it a new and deeper understanding of a wonderful and often misunderstood saying from the Gospel which hitherto had only awakened in me feelings of strong opposition: "And unto him that smiteth thee on the one cheek offer also the other" (St. Luke vi, 29). A wolf has enlightened me: not so that your enemy may strike you again do you turn the other cheek toward him, but to make him unable to do it.

KONRAD LORENZ

Biologist Konrad Lorenz (1903–89), who won a Nobel Prize in 1973, was well-known for the beauty and grace of his writing as well as for his development of the science of comparative ethology.

Things in Their Identity

A tree gives glory to God by being a tree. For in being what God means it to be it is obeying Him. It "consents," so to speak, to His creative love. It is expressing an idea which is in God and which is not distinct from the essence of God, and therefore a tree imitates God by being a tree.

The more a tree is like itself, the more it is like Him. If it tried to be like something else which it was never intended to be, it would be less like God and therefore it would give Him less glory.

No two created beings are exactly alike. And their individuality is no imperfection. On the contrary, the perfection of each created thing is not merely in its conformity to an abstract type but in its own individual identity with itself. This particular tree will give glory to God by spreading out its roots in the earth and raising its branches into the air and the light in a way that no other tree before or after it ever did or will do.

Do you imagine that the individual created things in the world are imperfect attempts at reproducing an ideal type which the Creator never quite succeeded in actualizing on earth? If that is so they do not give Him glory but proclaim that He is not a perfect Creator.

Therefore each particular being, in its individuality, its concrete nature and entity, with all its own characteristics and its private qualities and its own inviolable identity, gives glory to God by being precisely what He wants it to be here and now, in the circumstances ordained for it by His Love and His infinite Art.

The forms and individual characters of living and growing things, of inanimate beings, of animals and flowers and all nature, constitute their holiness in the sight of God.

Their inscape is their sanctity. It is the imprint of His wisdom and His reality in them.

The special clumsy beauty of this particular colt on this April day in this field under these clouds is a holiness created to God by His own creative wisdom and it declares the glory of God.

The pale flowers of the dogwood outside this window are saints. The little yellow flowers that nobody notices on the edge of that road are saints looking up into the face of God.

This leaf has its own texture and its own pattern of veins and its own holy shape, and the bass and trout hiding in the deep pools of the river are canonized by their beauty and their strength.

The lakes hidden among the hills are saints, and the sea too is a saint who praises God without interruption in her majestic dance.

The great, gashed, half-naked mountain is another of God's saints. There is no other like him. He is alone in his own character; nothing else in the world ever did or ever will imitate God in quite the same way. This is his sanctity.

THOMAS MERTON

Thomas Merton (1915–68) lived a life of paradox. A Trappist monk, he was a contemplative who craved solitude; at the same time he was a prolific author of essays, poetry, and critical studies who maintained a passion for social justice. In the 1960s, Merton developed deep friendships with prominent peace activists and civil rights activists. He also became deeply interested in eastern religions without relinquishing the integrity of his Christian faith.

Measuring the Depth

As I was desirous to recover the long lost bottom of Walden Pond, I surveyed it carefully, before the ice broke up, early in '46, with compass and chain and sounding line. There have been many stories told about the bottom, or rather no bottom, of this pond, which certainly had no foundation for themselves. It is remarkable how long men will believe in the bottomlessness of a pond without taking the trouble to sound it.

❧

When I had mapped the pond by the scale of ten rods to an inch, and put down the soundings, more than a hundred in all, I observed this remarkable coincidence. Having noticed that the number indicating the greatest depth was apparently in the center of the map, I laid a rule on the map lengthwise, and then breadthwise, and found, to my surprise, that the line of greatest length intersected the line of greatest breadth exactly at the point of greatest depth, notwithstanding that the middle is so nearly level, the outline of the pond far from regular, and the extreme length and breadth were got by measuring into the coves; and I said to myself, Who knows but this hint would conduct to the deepest part of the ocean as well as of a pond or puddle?

❧

What I have observed of the pond is no less true in ethics. . . . Draw lines through the length and breadth of the aggregate of a man's particular daily behaviors and waves of life into his coves and inlets, and where they intersect will be the height or depth of his character. Perhaps we need only to know how his shores trend and his adjacent country or circumstances, to infer his depth and concealed bottom.

HENRY DAVID THOREAU

In the winter of 1846, Henry David Thoreau (1817–62) surveyed the bottom of Walden Pond before the ice broke up and discovered, to his surprise, that the greatest depth of the pond was to be found not in the center, as he had expected, but at the intersection of the lines of greatest length and greatest width. From this startling discovery, he drew a lesson for sounding the depths of one's character.

Owning the Sky

Being thankful is an important part of the Medicine. In the traditional Cherokee Way, when children argued over an object, it was taken away from them and they were then encouraged to lie down on Mother Earth and look up at the sky. While observing the sky, the children were reminded that focusing attention on an object and on wanting to possess that object removed them from the harmony and balance of the Greater Circle. Then the children were asked to focus their attention on Father Sky. "Look at the sky. . . . Can you see the clouds?" the children might be asked. "Watch the way they move and change before your eyes. Can you see pictures in the clouds? Can you see the spirit people there?"

The focus of the children's attention with possessing something was replaced with the openness of the sky and the movement of all our relations in Galun'lati, or the Above World, such as the clouds, the wind, the birds. "Should we seek to own the sky?" it might have been asked. A renewed sense of relation and clarity was sought for the children as they were asked to open their minds and hearts to the movement and language of the cloud people, who speak in shapes and pictures.

The children might then have been asked to help out with a particular task as a way of replacing "wanting" thoughts with "giving" thoughts. This was only one of many ways in which to encourage openness, creativity, and humility in the presence of all Creation. This was a very important experience for helping young people (and some adults) to understand the power of relation and the sense of humility required to live in harmony and balance with all living beings in the Circle. True wisdom comes to us when we let go of the attachments that bind us and draw upon the sacred Medicine of all our relations. This, too, is Good Medicine.

MICHAEL TLANUSTA GARRETT

Michael Tlanusta Garrett grew up on the Cherokee Indian Reservation in the mountains of North Carolina. He has worked with Native American children and adolescents in the schools and in an urban Indian center. Currently, he is a professor of counselor education at the University of North Carolina at Charlotte and the author of *Walking on the Wind: Cherokee Teachings for Harmony and Balance* (1998) and the co-author, with his father, of *Medicine of the Cherokee: The Way of Right Relationship* (1996).

A Season for Swallows

Before spending another summer in Maine, I went up early, toward the end of
April, in order to dig a vegetable garden. There is a small barn close by the house
where in previous years barn and cliff swallows had nested in the loft along the
rafters, but they were past due when I arrived. Our neighbor told me that a few
pair had been flying in and out of her toolshed, but were not satisfied with it as a
place to nest. "Nervous about it" was the way she put it. Their problem was lack of
access to the barn. They had been coming in each spring through some broken holes
in the glass of two old window frames high on the north end, but I had boarded
those up in the autumn.

So I climbed up into the loft and took out the boards, and almost at once, as I
was climbing down again, four barn swallows flew in, filling the barn with their
warbly chatter. A whole new realm of talk and feeling had moved in, a world that in
spite of all the years I had watched the passing swallows was largely unknown to
me. What were all these low buzzy sounds and higher twitterings all about? Did
they have to do with claiming territory, urging each other on to nest, irritation at
my presence, or simply the satisfaction of having arrived? In any case it was a pleasure to listen to, like the talk of some cheerful and urgent company moving in on a
person who has been too long alone.

These four, with their tribal talk, were of a race that can travel all the way from
the latitude of the Yukon to Brazil or Argentina. Their return to the nesting places
where they grew up, or where they nested before, ties immense distances together.
As it is with the terns, thousands of miles of directive knowledge and memory are
in those little frames that can home in on a few yards of territory.

When I let the swallows in I felt as if I had let in earth's hunger. I had relieved
some of the pressures of primary need, and at the same time I was struck with how
much we block out. It is not only a matter of our overwhelming ability to destroy
life, but the extent to which we do not allow it to materialize. The boards against
the windows are of our manufacture, which may have all kinds of implications
about the human dilemma and the pity of it, but, more important, we should not
forget to take them off when it is time.

JOHN HAY

Born in 1915, naturalist John Hay lives in Cape Cod. He is the author of *The Great Beach*
(1963), *The Undiscovered Country* (1981), *A Beginner's Faith in Things Unseen* (1995), and others.

What Horses Can Teach Us

Examining different animals' social behavior in groups can help us become aware of our own inner (instinctive) affiliations and styles of communicating. We can use the dynamic interplay between herds, flocks and packs as a model for sorting out and solving our own difficult dynamics. For example, we can ask, "What is my orientation here?" and "Do I identify with the herd, the flock or the pack? What about the people around me? Where do they fit in?" Acting out these various roles can prove enlightening.

We've noticed that today fewer people display a herd-type orientation to life. Instead, what we see more of is the relationship of predator/prey. This serious social imbalance is characterized by a cat-and-mouse dynamic, which is one reason criminal activity has become an increasingly prevalent pastime. To restore a sense of order and safety within our communities, we need to correct our direction and regain equilibrium.

In non-threatening situations, a horse is capable of showing great affection and love. The horse shifts to aggression when confronted by an aggressor, then reverts to a basically loving nature when there is no danger present. A horse is capable of drawing upon both sides of its nature.

Unfortunately, humans have not developed the facility to shift between these two energies, nor have we made a concerted effort to hone our powers of perception. Consequently, we tend to operate through life on "automatic pilot." In our

state of blunted awareness, we behave something like sheep. We fail to see what goes on around us, or we deny what we see.

The mistrust we have in our intuitive abilities leaves us, like sheep, extremely vulnerable.

ADELE VON RÜST MCCORMICK,
MARLENA DEBORAH MCCORMICK

Adele von Rüst McCormick and Marlena Deborah McCormick have worked as psychotherapists for more than thirty years. While working with severely disturbed youths, they discovered the best healers were their herd of Peruvian Paso horses. Patients, they discovered, could learn more quickly on a horse than in a therapist's office. As a result, they founded the Three Eagles Equine Experience which uses horsemanship as a means to spirituality and connection with God.

What the Prairie Teaches Us

The prairie, although plain, inspires awe. It teaches us that grandeur can be wide as well as tall.

Young prairie plants put down deep roots first; only when these have been established do the plants invest much energy in growth above ground. They teach us that the work that matters doesn't always show.

Diversity makes the prairie resilient. One hundred acres of prairie may support three thousand species of insects alone, each of them posed to exploit—often beneficially—certain plants, microclimates, soils, weather conditions, and seasons. This exuberance equips the prairie to make the most of every opportunity, to meet every natural contingency. The prairie teaches us to see our own living arrangements as stingy and to understand that this miserliness is why they so frequently fall short of our expectations.

The prairie is a community. It is not just a landscape or the name of an area on a map, but a dynamic alliance of living plants, animals, birds, insects, reptiles, and micro-organisms, all depending upon each other. When too few of them remain, their community loses its vitality and they perish together. The prairie teaches us that our strength is in our neighbors. The way to destroy a prairie is to cut it up into tiny pieces, spaced so that they have no communication.

The prairie is patient. When drought sets in, as it inevitable does, prairie grasses bide their time. They do not flower without the nourishment to make good seed. Instead, they save their resources for another year when the rains have fallen, the seeds promise to be fat, and the earth is moist and ready to receive them. The prairie teaches us to save our energies for the opportune moment.

The prairie grows richer as it ages. Our own horticultural practices eventually deplete the soils. The top-soil washes or blows away; without additives, fertility dwindles. But the soils beneath the protective cover of prairie sod deepen over time; their tilth improves as burrowing animals and insects plow organic matter into them; fires recycle nutrients; deep roots bring up trace elements from the substrate; abundant legumes and microorganisms help to keep it fertile. The prairie was so effective at this work that, more than a century after it was broken, it remains the richest agricultural region in the world. The prairie teaches us how to be competitive without also being destructive.

The prairie is tolerant. There are thousands of species of living things on the prairie, but few of them are natives. The prairie has welcomed strangers of every kind and has borrowed ideas from all of its neighboring communities. In doing so, it has discovered how to flourish in a harsh place. The prairie teaches us to see the virtue of ideas not our own and the possibilities that new-comers bring.

The prairie turns adversity to advantage. Fires were frequent on the unplowed prairies. The prairie so completely adapted to this fact that is now requires fire for its health. Regular burning discourages weedy competitors, releases nutrients captured in leaves and stems, reduces thatch that would otherwise become a stifling mulch, stimulates cloning in grasses, and encourages the growth of legumes, which capture nitrogen from the air and make it available to the whole prairie community. The prairie teaches us to consider the uses that may be made of our setbacks.

The prairie is cosmopolitan. On the wings of winds and of birds, in the migrations of animals and insects, down the waters of streams and rivers come the messages, mainly contained in genetic codes, that sustain the prairie. Its storms swoop out of the Arctic or sweep up from the Gulf; many of its songbirds are familiar with the tropical rainforests; its monarch butterflies winter in the highlands of Mexico; its ducks vacation on seacoasts and in desert oases; its parasites hitchhike upon all of them. We think that we have discovered the global village, but the prairie knew of it a millennia ago.

The prairie is bountifully utilitarian. But it is lovely too, in a hundred thousand ways and in a million details, many of them so finely wrought that one must drop to one's knees to appreciate them. This is what, over all else, the prairie teaches us: there need be no contradiction between utility and beauty.

PAUL GRUCHOW

Born in 1947, Paul Gruchow grew up on a farm in rural Minnesota. As a child, Gruchow dreamed of living in the wilderness, as a hermit or a trapper. As an adult, Gruchow has communicated his love for nature through his writing and teaching. He is the author of *Journal of a Prairie Year* (1985), *The Necessity of Empty Spaces* (1988), *Grass Roots: The Universe of Home* (1995), *Boundary Waters: The Grace of the Wild* (1997), and *Worlds Within a World* (1999).

Lessons from Lao Tzu

In the world there is nothing more submissive and weak than water. Yet for attacking that which is hard and strong nothing can surpass it. This is because there is nothing that can take its place.

> *That the weak overcomes the strong,*
> *And the submissive overcomes the hard,*
> *Everyone in the world knows yet no one can put this*
> *knowledge into practice.*

(FROM BOOK II, CHAPTER 55)

The reason why the River and the Sea are able to be king of the hundred valleys is that they excel in taking the lower position. Hence they are able to be king of the hundred valleys.

> *Therefore, desiring to rule over the people,*
> *One must in one's words humble oneself before them;*
> *And, desiring to lead the people,*
> *One must, in one's person, follow behind them.*

(FROM BOOK II, CHAPTER 66)

The *Lao-tzu,* the classic book of Taoism, comes from the golden age of Chinese thought. Some have said that Lao Tzu was an older contemporary of Confucius; other scholars believe that Lao Tzu was not a historical figure at all, but that the book, *Lao-tzu,* is an ancient collection of wise sayings from various sources. The *Lao-tzu* actually consists of two books, the "Tao ching" (Book I) and the "Te ching" (Book II), in which *tao* means "way" and *te* means "virtue."

The Trailing Arbutus

I wandered lonely where the pine-trees made
Against the bitter East their barricade,
   And, guided by its sweet
Perfume, I found, within a narrow dell,
The trailing spring flower tinted like a shell
   Amid dry leaves and mosses at my feet.

From under dead boughs, for whose loss the pines
Moaned ceaseless overhead, the blossoming vines
   Lifted their glad surprise,
While yet the bluebird smoothed in leafless trees
His feathers ruffled by the chill seabreeze,
   And snow-drifts lingered under April skies.

And pausing, o'er the lonely flower I bent,
I thought of lives thus lowly, clogged and pent,
   Which yet find room,
Through care and cumber, coldness and decay,
To lend a sweetness to the ungenial day,
   And make the sad earth happier for their bloom.

JOHN GREENLEAF WHITTIER

Trailing arbutus, also known as Mayflower, is found throughout the eastern two-thirds of the United States, and is one of the first plants to flower in the spring. A very slow-growing, slightly woody plant, it spreads along the ground and is often concealed by leaves and mosses. Because it is so easily uprooted, it has disappeared in many places where it once flourished. Because of its unique qualities, trailing arbutus has inspired many writers, such as John Greenleaf Whittier (1807–92), a Quaker poet who worked vigorously for the abolition of slavery in the United States.

Of Algae and Clams

Certain animals in the sea live by becoming part-animal, part-plant. They engulf algae, which then establish themselves as complex plant tissues, essential for the life of the whole company. I suppose the giant clam, if he had more of a mind, would have moments of dismay on seeing what he as done to the plant world, incorporating so much of it, enslaving green cells, living off the photosynthesis. But the plant cells would take a different view of it, having captured the clam on the most satisfactory of terms, including the small lenses in his tissues that focus sunlight for their benefit; perhaps algae have bad moments about what they may collectively be doing to the world of clams.

With luck, our own situation might be similar, on a larger scale. This might turn out to be a special phase in the morphogenesis of the earth when it is necessary to have something like us, for a time anyway, to fetch and carry energy, look after new symbiotic arrangements, store up information for some future season, do a certain amount of ornamenting, maybe even carry seeds around the solar system. That kind of thing. Handyman for the earth.

I would much prefer this useful role, if I had any say, to the essentially unearthly creature we seem otherwise on the way of becoming. It would mean making some quite fundamental changes in our attitudes toward each other, if we were really to think of ourselves as indispensable elements of nature. We would surely become the environment to worry about the most. We would discover, in ourselves, the sources of wonderment and delight that we have discerned in all other manifestations of nature. . . .

LEWIS THOMAS

Lewis Thomas (1913–93) received his M.D. from Harvard and was known both for his writing and for his contributions to medicine. Dr. Thomas served as a research pathologist and as president of the Memorial Sloan-Kettering Cancer Center in New York. This selection comes from his book, *Lives of a Cell: Notes of a Biology Watcher,* which won the National Book Award.

Practicing the Virtue of Justice

1. "Each particular being, in its individuality," writes Thomas Merton, "gives glory to God by being precisely what He wants it to be here and now." Practice seeing someone close to you with that sort of perspective. In other words, try to see that person's individual identity as God sees that person, and not as you might like that person to be.

2. Meditate on this injunction for living from the book of Micah (6:8): "What does the Lord require of you? To act justly and to love mercy and to walk humbly with your God." Consider how your actions might be directed by these three requirements.

3. Paul Gruchow shows what the prairie, with its rich interconnections, can "teach" us. Choose any ecosystem which appeals to you (e.g., a forest, a wetland, a desert), and study that ecosystem so that you understand the interconnectedness of that place. Then, in a way similar to Gruchow's, reflect on what that ecosystem can teach you.

4. In the traditional Cherokee Way, Michael Garrett tells us, children who argued over an object were told to lie down and look up at the sky, to open their hearts and minds by considering, "Should we seek to own the sky?" Such contemplation, followed by a task of helping, was an important experience in understanding community relations. Create your own approach to this Cherokee exercise, especially when you are feeling the tension of owning things.

5. A bird or an animal, Barbara Kingsolver shows us, may protect its territory; but it doesn't seek to own it: it doesn't post a "no trespassing" sign. Consider how you might more generously share your space, with other species or with other people. How might you intentionally practice a greater degree of peaceful coexistence?

6. In order to judge the depth of someone's character, consider employing Henry David Thoreau's imaginative strategy, which he got from surveying the depth of Walden pond. Visualize the shape of that individual's life as a pond; draw, or imagine, the contours of that individual's daily behaviors and habits, including all the irregularities of that life, the "coves and inlets" of behavior, the digressions, the departures from symmetry. Factor these things into your consideration of that person, don't rule

them out. Then, when you imaginatively draw lines through the length and width of that shape, see if you might not discover a greater depth than anticipated, or in a spot unexpected. Thoreau suggests: "perhaps we need only to know how his shores trend . . . to infer his depth and concealed bottom."

7. Look for the trailing arbutus, the beauty to be found beneath dry leaves and mosses at your feet. Consider, as John Greenleaf Whittier does, the lives it represents.

Faith

Nature's Instruction
for Living in Trust

FAITH IS THE MOST PROBLEMATIC OF THE VIRTUES, for there seems to be so much at stake. We might overlook intemperance, accept a lack of fortitude, or even understand a loss of hope. But "without faith," says the writer to the Hebrews, "it is impossible to please God" (Hebrews 11:6). To lose one's faith, some would say, is to lose one's soul.

Faith, the nineteenth century romantics believed, could be renewed through nature. "In the woods we return to reason and faith," taught the American sage, Ralph Waldo Emerson. Indeed, the woods seemed to be the most fitting place for worship. "The groves were God's first temple," sang William Cullen Bryant in "A Forest Hymn" of 1825.

> *Be it ours to meditate,*
> *In these calm shades, thy milder majesty,*
> *And to the beautiful order of thy works*
> *Learn to conform the order of our lives.*

The belief that one could read the lessons of eternity on the works of nature, and conform one's life accordingly, was central to these romantics; and that belief has also been compatible with Christian doctrine. St. Paul, in his epistle to the Romans, taught: "since the creation of the world God's invisible qualities—his eternal power and divine nature—have been clearly seen, being understood from what has been made" (Romans 1:20). Nineteenth century Americans found they could respond to the new "gospel" of Nature without rejecting the Bible. America, as historian Perry Miller explained, "could even more energetically proclaim itself Christian and cherish the churches; but it could derive its inspiration from the mountains, the lakes, the forests" *(Errand into the Wilderness)*.

Sometimes Christians hesitate to trust the connections between nature and faith. Charles Haddon Spurgeon, the great English preacher, frequently assured his students not to shun the book of nature. "You need never feel any qualms of conscience about using the facts of nature to illustrate the truths of Scripture," he insisted. "When you use natural history to illustrate the Scriptures, you are only explaining one of God's books by another volume that He has written."

John Muir, who founded the Sierra Club and was instrumental in preserving Yosemite, grew up in a fundamentalist Christian home and incurred the fierce disapproval of his father for delighting in nature. "You cannot warm the heart of the saint of God with your cold icy-topped mountains," his father wrote to John. "O, my dear son, come away from them to the spirit of God and His holy word, and He will show our lovely Jesus unto you, who is by His finished work presented to you, without money and price" *(To Yosemite and Beyond)*.

Muir, however, found in nature the warmth that was never present in his father's icy faith. Muir "saw in nature attributes which Christians see in Christ," explains Presbyterian minister Richard Austin in his book, *Baptized Into Wilderness: A Christian Perspective on John Muir*.

The most conspicuous image of Christ Muir found was the Sequoia, the "tree of life," as he called it. "The King tree & me have sworn eternal love," he wrote in 1870:

> I wish I was so drunk and Sequoical that I could preach the green-brown woods to all the juiceless world, descending from this divine wilderness like a John Baptist eating Douglass Squirrels and wild honey or wild anything, crying, Repent for the Kingdom of Sequoia is at hand.
>
> There is a balm in these leafy Gileads...; Come Suck Sequoia and be saved. *(The Pathless Way)*

Some might see Muir's rhetoric as sacrilegious, but it's rather pure ecstasy. Muir's imagination was stirred not only by the Sequoia's tremendous height and grandeur and longevity but also by its life-giving streams: "The roots of this immense tree fill the ground, forming a sponge which hoards the bounty of the clouds and sends it forth in clear perennial streams," he explained in his essay "The Sequoia" *(Our National Parks)*. It is "a tree of life, a never-failing spring, sending living water to the lowlands all through the hot, rainless summer."

Muir drew upon Biblical language naturally, just as Christ used natural metaphors to describe himself. Imagining Christ, the leafy Balm of Gilead, as a giant Sequoia gave a new dimension to his worship. "This glorious valley might well be called a church," wrote Muir to his brother, "for every lover of the great Creator who comes within the broad overwhelming influences of the place fails not to worship as they never did before" *(To Yosemite and Beyond)*.

It may be impossible in the twenty-first century ever to regain a sense of nature as a cathedral or sanctuary. We are more likely to be found dropping by the mall than stopping by the woods. Still, the world is charged with the grandeur of God, and can ignite faith.

Jesus frequently expressed astonishment that some could have so little faith while others had so much. "Your faith has healed you," he would say to ordinary people who sought him out (Matthew 9:22). More often he was chiding his disciples, "O you of little faith" (Matthew 6:30).

On one such occasion, he turned to nature. "Look at the birds of the air," he urged (Matthew 6:26). "See how the lilies of the field grow. . . .

> "I tell you that not even Solomon in all his splendor was dressed like one of these. If that is how God clothes the grass of the field, which is here today and tomorrow is thrown into the fire, will he not much more clothe you, O you of little faith? So do not worry, saying, 'What shall we eat?' or 'What shall we drink?' or 'What shall we wear?'" (Matthew 6:28-31)

Some appreciate this lesson as an illustration of faith. Be like the birds; be like the lilies. They don't worry; neither should you. Faith is an absence of worry. Faith simply accepts God's provision.

It may be more fruitful to see Christ's instruction as an *invitation* to faith rather than an *illustration* of faith. His challenge is to "consider." Ponder the examples of the lilies and the birds. Consider also the blind faith of a honeysuckle shoot. Consider the delicate, snowy egret that roosts with dung-scratching chickens. Consider the dragonfly's lip. Assess the evidence; attend to their significance. Witness God's care, extravagance, exuberance, wildness. . . . Approached this way, faith is not merely blind trust, but an exercise of imagination's grasp.

Faith, the Scriptures tell us, "is being sure of what we hope for and certain of what we do not see" (Hebrews 11:1). "Faith is understanding's step," said Augustine; "and understanding is faith's reward." It is "God felt by the heart, not by reason," in Pascal's words. To Martin Luther, there were two kinds of faith: "There is a faith which believes what is said of God is true; there is a faith which throws itself on God." Charles Spurgeon put it simply: "True faith in its very essence rests in this—a leaning on Christ."

In the selections that follow, nature still has the power to awaken faith. Some of the writers here consider creation through eyes of a romantic sensibility in which everything fits; others have more of a postmodern consciousness where things don't always fit. All, however, strive to make us certain of what we do not see; and sometimes to see ourselves anew through the eyes of faith.

The Faith of a Vine

Whenever I look over my right shoulder, as I sit at my desk writing these sentences, I see a long shoot of a honeysuckle that came in through a crack of my imperfectly closed window last summer. It came in looking, or rather feeling, for something to cling to. It first dropped down upon a pile of books, then reached off till it struck the window-sill of another large window; along this it crept, its regular leaves standing up like so many pairs of green ears, looking very pretty. Coming to the end of the open way there, it turned to the left and reached out into vacancy, till it struck another window-sill running at right angles to the former; along this it traveled nearly half an inch a day, till it came to the end of that road. Then it ventured out into vacant space again, and pointed straight toward me at my desk, ten feet distant. Day by day it kept its seat upon the window-sill, and stretched out farther and farther, almost beckoning me to give it a lift or to bring it support. I could hardly resist its patient daily appeal. Late in October it had bridged about three feet of the distance that separated us, when, one day, the moment came when it could maintain itself outright in the air no longer, and it fell to the floor. "Poor thing," I said, "your faith was blind, but it was real. You knew there was a support somewhere, and you tried all ways to find it." This is Nature. She goes around the circle, she tries every direction, sure that she will find a way at some point. Animals in cages behave in a similar way, looking for a means of escape. In the vine-yard I see the grape-vines reaching out blindly in all directions for some hold for their tendrils. The young arms seize upon one another and tighten their hold as if they had at last found what they were in search of. Stop long enough beside one of the vines, and it will cling to you and run all over you.

JOHN BURROUGHS

"If we do not go to church so much as did our fathers," wrote John Burroughs (1837–1921), "we go to the woods much more, and are much more inclined to make a temple of them than they were." Burroughs wrote about nature clearly and directly, and is credited with developing nature writing as a vibrant literary form, publishing more than twenty-five books.

The Bat

I was reading about rationalism,
the kind of thing we do up north
in early winter, where the sun
leaves work for the day at 4:15.

Maybe the world is intelligible
to the rational mind:
and maybe we light the lamps at dusk
for nothing....

Then I heard wings overhead.

The cats and I chased the bat
in circles—living room, kitchen,
pantry, kitchen, living room....
At every turn it evaded us

Like the identity of the third person
in the Trinity: the one
who spoke through the prophets,
the one who astounded Mary
by suddenly coming near.

JANE KENYON

Until her untimely death from leukemia, Jane Kenyon (1947–95) lived with her poet husband, Donald Hall, on a farm in New Hampshire. Kenyon was educated at the University of Michigan, and published four volumes of poetry. Many of her poems are concerned with the rhythms and seasons of nature. Reviewing her work in the *New York Times,* poet Carol Muske said that Jane Kenyon "sees this world as a kind of threshold through which we enter God's wonder." This poem exemplifies that claim.

Take Something Like a Star

O Star (the fairest one in sight)
We grant your loftiness the right
To some obscurity of cloud—
It will not do to say of night,
Since dark is what brings out your light.
Some mystery becomes the proud.
But to be wholly taciturn
In your reserve is not allowed.
Say something to us we can learn
By heart and when alone repeat.
Say something! And it says, 'I burn.'
But say with what degree of heat.
Talk Fahrenheit, talk Centigrade.
Use language we can comprehend.
Tell us what elements you blend.
It gives us strangely little aid,
But does tell something in the end.
And steadfast as Keats' Eremite,
Not even stooping from its sphere,
It asks a little of us here.
It asks of us a certain height,
So when at times the mob is swayed
To carry praise or blame too far,
We may take something like a star
To stay our minds on and be staid.

ROBERT FROST

Robert Frost (1874–1963), who spent most of his life in New England, was perhaps America's most beloved poet of the twentieth century. Many remember his reading at the Presidential inauguration of John F. Kennedy in 1961. A good poem, he maintained, "begins in delight and ends in wisdom." Frost was also an amateur astronomer and composed a number of poems about stars. Here, Frost alludes to another poem about stars, John Keats' "Bright Star" (1819). There are numerous Biblical echoes throughout this poem by Frost, including Isaiah 26:3, "Thou wilt keep him in perfect peace, whose mind is stayed on thee" (KJV).

Redemption

Driving toward Malheur Lake in the Great Basin of south-eastern Oregon, I saw a coyote. I stopped the car, opened the door, and walked toward him.

It was another crucifixion in the West, a hide hung on a barbed-wire fence with a wrangler's prayer: Cows are sacred. Sheep, too. No trespassing allowed. The furred skin was torn with ragged edges, evidence that it had been pulled away from the dog-body by an angry hand and a dull knife.

Standing in the middle of the High Desert, cumulus clouds pulled my gaze upward. I thought about Coyote Butte, a few miles south, how a person can sit on top between two sage-covered ears and watch a steady stream of western tanagers fly through during spring migration; yellow bodies, black wings, red heads.

And how a few miles west near Foster Flats, one can witness dancing grouse on their ancestral leks, even in rain, crazy with desire, their booming breasts mimicking the sound of water.

Down the road, I watched a small heard of pronghorn on the other side of the fence, anxiously running back and forth parallel to the barbed wire, unable to jump. Steens Mountain shimmered above the sage flats like a ghost.

My eyes returned to Jesus Coyote, stiff on his cross, savior of our American rangelands. We can try and kill all that is native, string it up by its hind legs for all to see, but spirit howls and wildness endures.

Anticipate resurrection.

TERRY TEMPEST WILLIAMS

Terry Tempest Williams was born in 1955 to a Mormon family with roots in Utah since 1847. She currently serves as Naturalist-in-Residence at the Utah Museum of Natural History in Salt Lake City. Her writing frequently seeks to reveal the spiritual dimension of the natural world. In this selection, she also suggests an untamable wildness about Jesus. Williams' most popular book, *Refuge: An Unnatural History of Family and Place* (1991) ponders the necessity of healing between humans and nature.

Consider

Consider
The lilies of the field, whose bloom is brief—
    We are as they;
    Like them we fade away,
        As doth a leaf.

Consider
The sparrows of the air, of small account:
    Our God doth view
    Whether they fall or mount—
        He guards us too.

Consider
The lilies, that do neither spin nor toil,
    Yet are most fair—
    What profits all this care,
        And all this coil?

Consider
The birds, that have no barn nor harvest-weeks:
    God gives them food—
    Much more our Father seeks
        To do us good.

CHRISTINA ROSSETTI

Christina Rossetti (1830–94), a poet associated with the Pre-Raphaelite movement in England, was a devout Anglican whose life was dedicated to the care of her relatives and to charity. Although troubled by bouts of ill health, she published several collections of poetry in her lifetime including *Goblin Market* and *The Prince's Progress.* This poem is based upon the teachings of Jesus as recorded in Luke 12:22-28.

The Creator's Exuberance

The world is full of creatures that for some reason seem stranger to us than others, and libraries are full of books describing them—hagfish, platypuses, lizardlike pangolins four feet long with bright green, lapped scales like umbrella-tree leaves on a bush hut roof, butterflies emerging from anthills, spiderlings wafting through the air clutching tiny silken balloons, horseshoe crabs . . . the creator creates. Does he stoop, does he speak, does he save, succor, prevail? Maybe. But he creates; he creates everything and anything.

Of all the known forms of life, only about ten percent are still living today. All other forms—fantastic plants, ordinary plants, living animals with unimaginably various wings, tails, teeth, brains—are utterly and forever gone. That is a great many forms that have been created. Multiplying ten times the number of living forms today yields a profusion that is quite beyond what I consider thinkable. Why so many forms? Why not just that one hydrogen atom? The creator goes off on one wild, specific tangent after another, or millions simultaneously, with an exuberance that would seem to be unwarranted, and with an abandoned energy sprung from an unfathomable font. What is going on here? The point of the dragonfly's terrible lip, the giant water bug, birdsong, or the beautiful dazzle and flash of sunlighted minnows, is not that it all fits together like clockwork—for it doesn't, particularly, not even inside the goldfish bowl—but that it all flows so freely wild, like the creek, that it all surges in such a free, fringed tangle. Freedom is the world's water and weather, the world's nourishment freely given, its soil and sap: and the creator loves pizzazz.

Annie Dillard

"Sometimes I ride a bucking faith while one hand grips and the other flails in the air," writes Annie Dillard near the end of *Pilgrim at Tinker Creek*. That book won the Pulitzer Prize in 1975. Her subsequent books include *Holy the Firm* (1977), *Teaching a Stone to Talk* (1982), *An American Childhood* (1987), *The Writing Life* (1989), and *For the Time Being* (2000). Annie Dillard currently lives in Connecticut.

God's Grandeur

The world is charged with the grandeur of God.
   It will flame out, like shining from shook foil;
   It gathers to a greatness, like the ooze of oil
Crushed. Why do men then now not reck his rod?
Generations have trod, have trod, have trod:
   And all is seared with trade; bleared, smeared with toil;
   And wears man's smudge and shares man's smell: the soil
Is bare now, nor can foot feel, being shod.

And for all this, nature is never spent;
   There lives the dearest freshness deep down things;
And though the last lights off the black West went
   Oh, morning, at the brown brink eastward, springs—
Because the Holy Ghost over the bent
World broods with warm breast and with ah! bright wings.

GERARD MANLEY HOPKINS

Born near London, Gerard Manley Hopkins (1844–89) attended Oxford and originally planned to become a painter. But when he joined the Catholic Church at age 22, his plans changed, and shortly after, he decided to become a Jesuit. At age 40, he became professor of classics at University College in Dublin, but died of typhoid a few years later. His poetry was not collected and published until 1918.

God's Presence in Nature

I walked abroad alone, in a solitary place in my father's pasture, for contemplation. And as I was walking there, and looked up on the sky and clouds; there came into my mind a sweet sense of the glorious majesty and grace of God that I know not how to express. I seemed to see them both in a sweet conjunction, majesty and meekness joined together. It was a sweet and gentle, and holy majesty; and also a majestic meekness; an awful sweetness; a high, and great, and holy gentleness.

After this my sense of divine things gradually increased, and became more and more lively, and had more of that inward sweetness. The appearance of everything was altered: there seemed to be, as it were, a calm, sweet cast, or appearance of divine glory, in almost everything. God's excellency, his wisdom, his purity and love, seemed to appear in everything: in the sun, moon and stars; in the clouds, and blue sky; in the grass, flowers, trees; in the water, and all nature; which used greatly to fix my mind. I often used to sit and view the moon for a long time, and so in the daytime spent much time in viewing the clouds and sky to behold the sweet glory of God in these things, in the meantime, singing forth with a low voice my contemplations of the Creator and Redeemer. And scarce anything, among all the works of nature, was so sweet to me as thunder and lightning. Formerly, nothing had been so terrible to me. I used to be a person uncommonly terrified with thunder, and it used to strike me with terror when I saw a thunderstorm rising. But now, on the contrary, it rejoiced me. I felt God at the first appearance of a thunderstorm. And used to take the opportunity at such times to fix myself to view the clouds, and see the lightnings play, and hear the majestic and awful voice of God's thunder, which often times was exceeding entertaining, leading me to sweet contemplations of my great and glorious God. And while I viewed, used to spend my time, as it always seemed natural to me, to sing or chant forth my meditations, to speak my thoughts in soliloquies, and speak with a singing voice.

JONATHAN EDWARDS

Jonathan Edwards (1703–58) is usually remembered for his famous sermon, "Sinners in the Hands of an Angry God" (1741), which fueled the Great Awakening in New England. But Edward's contributions to theology and American philosophy were of more enduring significance. Edwards brought to Puritan theology a new appreciation of the natural world, as this passage from his *Personal Narrative* testifies.

God's Great Owl

He who would feel the earth spin and the planets circle must get away from human beings and all other living things; even from whatever suggests them. Just as in human company one can hardly be properly aware of the other manifestations of animate Nature, so in the presence of animate Nature herself one cannot properly be aware of what is older and perhaps more enduring than animate Nature; with what was before her and will perhaps continue to be, time without end, after the last restless protozoan is dead and the last lichen shriveled on the surviving rock. It should not be on a night of storm, for that is something which must be struggled against and resistance to anything is fatal. But if it be a night of quiet and moonlight and snow, the physical place need not be remote. All the worlds except the white, dead, gleaming one can disappear twenty-five feet from a warm, cozy house.

I remember very vividly one such evening. It was the unghostly hour of eight p.m. and I had gone down the path shoveled across my lawn toward the garage, only a few dozen yards away. Suddenly I was alone with the universe. The realest things besides myself in all existence were not either human beings nor any other living things. I seemed about to grasp what the earth, the suns, and the stars meant to themselves as distinguished from what they mean to any of us creatures—from the simplest to the most complex—who live and grow and then die; who seem to have to purchase our kind of awareness at the price of the agreement that it shall be brief.

Then, at that very moment, came the far-away hoot—bark, it had better be called—of one of the great owls. There are few lonesomer sounds made by any living thing, but no living thing can be lonesome as the stars and the snow are lonesome. I remembered once having heard that the owl hoots in order to frighten the cowering mice into betraying by a start their secret whereabouts. What I saw now in my mind's eye was the sudden pounce of the great bird, the shrill scream of the mouse, and then—after aggressor and victim had disappeared together—the tiny spot of blood staining the inhuman purity of the snow. In an instant I was back among my own kind. The communication from space was never received. Sometimes I wonder whether God, the only time He ever began to speak to me, was interrupted by one of His own owls.

JOSEPH WOOD KRUTCH

Joseph Wood Krutch (1893–1970) became one of America's most prolific nature writers and a highly-sought editor and mentor of other nature writers.

A Leaf of Grass

I believe a leaf of grass is no less than the journey-work of the stars,
And the pismire is equally perfect, and a grain of sand, and the egg of the wren,
And the tree-toad is a chef-d'oeuvre for the highest,
And the running blackberry would adorn the parlors of heaven,
And the narrowest hinge in my hand puts to scorn all machinery,
And the cow crunching with depress'd head surpasses any statue,
And a mouse is miracle enough to stagger sextillions of infidels.

WALT WHITMAN

In his poetic masterpiece, *Leaves of Grass,* Walt Whitman (1819–92) claims, "My faith is the greatest of faiths and the least of faiths." Unconventional in his thinking and in his poetic form, Whitman conceived of *Leaves of Grass* as a type of "American Bible," which would hearten and uplift its readers.

Only a Flower

Strange that the spring has come
On meadow and vale and hill,
For here in the sunless slum
My bosom is frozen still.
And I wear the wadded things
Of the dreary winter days,
But out of the heart of this little flower
God gazes into my face!

TOYOHIKO KAGAWA

Toyohiko Kagawa (1888–1960) was a well-known Christian social reformer in Japan. As a young man, he moved to the "sunless slum" of Kobe, referred to above, where he dedicated himself to fighting the social injustice and poverty he saw around him. In his work, Kagawa emphasized the significance of the cross as a symbol of love and of the acceptance of suffering.

Faith in a Resurrection

Everyone has heard the story which has gone the rounds of New England, of a strong and beautiful bug which came out of the dry leaf of an old table of apple-tree wood, which had stood in a farmer's kitchen for sixty years, first in Connecticut, and afterward in Massachusetts,—from an egg deposited in the living tree many years earlier still, as appeared by counting the annual layers beyond it; which was heard gnawing out for several weeks, hatched perchance by the heat of an urn. Who does not feel his faith in a resurrection and immortality strengthened by hearing of this? Who knows what beautiful and winged life, whose egg has been buried for ages under many concentric layers of woodenness in the dead dry life of society, deposited at first in the alburnum of the green and living tree, which has been gradually converted into the semblance of its well-seasoned tomb,—heard perchance gnawing out now for years by the astonished family of man, as they sat round the festive board,—may unexpectedly come forth from amidst society's most trivial and handselled furniture, to enjoy its perfect summer life at last!

HENRY DAVID THOREAU

With this anecdote, Henry David Thoreau (1817–62) concluded his masterpiece, *Walden*, an account of his two-year long experiment of living alone in the woods where he went to confront "the essential facts of life, and see if I could not learn what it had to teach." From his experience, he gained a vibrant belief in resurrection and immortality.

An Unexpected Lesson from a Spider

I once received an unexpected lesson from a spider.

It happened far away on a rainy morning in the West. I had come up a long gulch looking for fossils, and there, just at eye level, lurked a huge yellow-and-black orb spider, whose web was moored to the tall spears of buffalo grass at the edge of the arroyo. It was her universe, and her senses did not extend beyond the lines and spokes of the great wheel she inhabited. Her extended claws could feel every vibration throughout that delicate structure. She knew the tug of wind, the fall of a raindrop, the flutter of a trapped moth's wing. Down one spoke of the web ran a stout ribbon of gossamer on which she could hurry out to investigate her prey.

Curious, I took a pencil from my pocket and touched a strand of the web. Immediately there was a response. The web, plucked by its menacing occupant, began to vibrate until it was a blur. Anything that had brushed claw or wing against that amazing snare would be thoroughly entrapped. As the vibrations slowed, I could see the owner fingering her guidelines for signs of struggle. A pencil point was an intrusion into this universe for which no precedent existed. Spider was circumscribed by spider ideas; its universe was spider universe. All outside was irrational, extraneous, at best raw material for spider. As I proceeded on my way along the gully, like a vast impossible shadow, I realized that in the world of spider I did not exist.

❦

The spider was a symbol of man in miniature. The wheel of the web brought the analogy home clearly. Man, too, lies at the heart of a web, a web extending through the starry reaches of sidereal space, as well as backward into the dark realm of prehistory. His great eye upon Mount Palomar looks into a distance of millions of light-years, his radio ear hears the whisper of even more remote galaxies, he peers through the electron microscope upon the minute particles of his own being. It is a web no creature of earth has even spun before. Like the orb spider, man lies at the heart of it, listening. Knowledge has given him the memory of earth's history beyond the time of his emergence. Like the spider's claw, a part of him touches a world he will never enter in the flesh. Even now, one can see him reaching forward into time with new machines, computing, analyzing, until elements of the shadowy future will also compose part of the invisible web he fingers.

Yet still my spider lingers in memory against the sunset sky. Spider thoughts in a spider universe—sensitive to raindrop and moth flutter, nothing beyond, nothing allowed for the unexpected, the inserted pencil from the world outside.

Is man at heart any different from the spider, I wonder: man thoughts, as limited as spider thoughts, contemplating now the nearest star with the threat of bringing with him the fungus rot from earth, wars, violence, the burden of a population he refuses to control, cherishing again his dream of the Adamic Eden he had pursued and lost in the green forests of America. Now it beckons again like a mirage from beyond the moon. Let man spin his web, I thought further; it is his nature. But I considered also the work of the phagocytes swarming in the rivers of my body, the unresting cells in their mortal universe. What is it we are a part of that we do not see, as the spider was not gifted to discern my face, or my little probe into her world?

LOREN EISELEY

Loren Eiseley (1907–77) was born in Lincoln, Nebraska, and served as a professor of anthropology at the University of Pennsylvania for thirty years. He published numerous books of poetry, scientific articles and personal essays. Annie Dillard claims that Loren Eiseley "restored the essay's place in imaginative literature."

Sacrament

God, I have sought you as a fox seeks chickens,
Curbing my hunger with cunning.
The times I have tasted your flesh
There was no bread and wine between us,
Only night and the wind beating the grass.

ALDEN NOWLAN

Alden Nowlan (1933–83) was one of Canada's most popular Maritime poets who also worked as a journalist and playwright. Nowlan won numerous awards for such collections as *Bread, Wine, and Salt* (1967), *Playing the Jesus Game* (1971), and the drama, *Frakenstein: The Man Who Became God* (1974). Alden Nowlan lived and wrote in his beloved New Brunswick.

The Force of Spirit

I want a name for the force that keeps Earl McClure asking questions while the tide of life withdraws from him. I want a name for the force that abandoned the body of Dessa McClure and left it like a piece of shrouded furniture on a cart in the funeral home. I want a name for the force that carried a woman dying of cancer through her studies and across a stage to claim her diploma. I want a name for the force that binds me to Ruth, to her parents, to my parents, to our children, to neighbors and friends, to the land and all its creatures.

This power is larger than life, although it contains life. It's tougher than love, although it contains love. It's akin to the power I sense in lambs nudging the teats of their dams to bring down milk, in the raucous tumult of crows high in trees, in the splendor of leaves gorging on sun. I recognize this force at work in children puzzling over a new fact, in grown-ups welcoming strangers, in our capacity, young and old, for laughter and kindness, for mercy and imagination.

No name is large enough to hold this power, but of all the inadequate names the one that comes to me now is spirit. I know the risks of using such a church word. Believers may find me blasphemous for speaking of the wind that blows through all things without tracing the breath to God. Nonbelievers may find me superstitious for invoking any force beyond gravity, electromagnetism, and the binding energy of atoms. But I must run those risks, for I cannot understand the world, cannot understand my life, without appealing to the force of spirit. If what I feel for my wife or her father and mother is only a by-product of hormones, then what I feel for swift rivers or slow turtles, for the shivering call of a screech owl or the green thrust of bloodroot breaking ground, is equally foolish. If we and all the creatures who share the earth with us are only bundles of quarks in motion, however intricate or clever the shapes, then our affection for one another, our concern for other species, our devotion to wildness, our longing for union with the Creation are all mere delusions.

SCOTT RUSSELL SANDERS

Born in 1945, Scott Russell Sanders grew up in Tennessee and Ohio and was educated at Brown University and Cambridge University. The author of more than a dozen books, Sanders claims that his writing emphasizes "where we truly live—not inside a skull, a house, a town, or nation, not inside any human creation at all, but in the creation." Sanders is a distinguished professor at Indiana University. His recent works include *Staying Put: Making a Home in a Restless World* (1993), *Hunting for Hope* (1998), and *The Force of Spirit* (2000).

Surprised by the Sacred

My family moved to a farm in Missouri when I was fifteen. Along with the purchase of the farm, we inherited a herd of sheep, just at lambing season. It was a painfully cold, late January, and when twins were born, it was often necessary to bring one lamb into the house to keep it from freezing while the ewe mother took care of the other. Even today, many years later, I can see those newborn lambs, whiter and cleaner than the snow they lay on at birth, each so immediately out of the warm wet womb into the wide winter cold, the unfathomably deep, grey skies, the world wholly new to their eyes just opened, and, hanging from each lamb, the drying string of a bloody umbilical cord.

I've never felt anything again so soft as the fleecy silk of those young lambs, silk so soft it was barely discernible against my fingertips, the sensation enhanced by the feel of the thin, warm body beating beneath. I remember having one of my fingers accidentally mistaken for a nipple and taken quickly into a lamb's mouth, the surprisingly strong sucking and gripping power of that tongue and throat on my finger. Life is this final, the altogether everything, this crucial.

We seem to be creatures who need physical sensation, tangible objects to imbue with the abstractions that mean so much to us as a species—innocence, compassion, peace. Each of the newborn lambs we cared for during those early years of my adolescence has come to be for me the very feel, the sound, the living body of faith, of purity and hope. These are the same virtues that many people in the past believed were presented to God in the sacrifice of unblemished lambs. "Behold the Lamb of God," John the Baptist announces when he sees Christ walking toward him out of the crowd. The newborn lambs of my adolescence entered the world bearing this history in their being, in their bodies, stories of the sacred. And they were dear to me, their presence enhanced, because of the stories they bore.

PATTIANN ROGERS

Born in 1940 in Joplin, Missouri, poet Pattiann Rogers writes about the natural world with a precision and grace. She claims that many of her poems were influenced by her children and their curiosity, energy and closeness to the earth. Her numerous books include *The Expectations of Light* (1981), *Splitting and Binding* (1989), *Eating Bread and Honey* (1997) and *The Dream of the Marsh Wren: Writing as Reciprocal Creation* (1999).

In Whom We Live and Move and Have Our Being

Birds afloat in air's current,
sacred breath? No, not breath of God,
it seems, but God
the air enveloping the whole
globe of being.
It's we who breathe, in, out, in, the sacred,
leaves astir, our wings
rising, ruffled—but only the saints
take flight. We cower
in cliff-crevice or edge out gingerly
on branches close to the nest. The wind
marks the passage of holy ones riding
that ocean of air. Slowly their wake
reaches us, rocks us.
But storm or still,
numb or poised in attention,
we inhale, exhale, inhale,
encompassed, encompassed.

DENISE LEVERTOV

American poet Denise Levertov (1923–97) was born in England to a Welsh mother and a Jewish father who had converted to Christianity, but maintained a vibrant interest in Hasidism. Denise Levertov became well known as a political poet during the years of the Vietnam War. Her later poems began to express her Christian faith more openly. Near the end of her life, she said: "I've come to see certain analogies, and also some interaction, between the journey of art and the journey of faith."

Practicing the Virtue of Faith

1. Consider one of the various definitions of *faith* from the introduction to this chapter, or compose a one-sentence definition of your own. Embrace this definition and meditate on its implications for your life.

2. Gerard Manley Hopkins says that the world is "charged with the grandeur of God" that will "flame out." Jane Kenyon writes of the sudden appearance of the bat, that reminds her of the Holy Spirit. Be on the alert for the sudden, flaming, appearances of God's grandeur in the weary world around you.

3. Read the Biblical history in Hebrews 11 of those people who stepped out "by faith." Note their specific actions of faith described: offered, built, traveled, trusted, hid, endured, etc. In what specific way do you need to "step out" by faith? What action would you like to say, "By faith, I _____"? Pray for this deliberate faith.

4. "Faith comes from hearing the message, and the message is heard through the word of God" (Romans 10:17). Trust this claim. Try simply listening, long and attentively, to the message—whether through the Bible or through the book of nature.

5. Terry Tempest Williams sees an image of Jesus Christ in the crucified coyote. John Muir contemplates the giant Sequoia as a symbol of Christ. Pattiann Rogers recalls the Lamb of God. If you are a Christian, find a natural image that represents Christ for you. Dwell on the qualities of this natural form, and allow it to speak of Christ to you.

6. "In the woods we return to reason and faith," wrote Emerson in the nineteenth century. Others have experienced a sense of the eternal beside streams, in pastures, in a slum. Find a place where you have a keen sense of God's presence. Retreat there often for prayer and listening.

7. Annie Dillard reminds us that the Creator "is apt to create anything." Go to a zoo, an aquarium, a museum of natural history, or anywhere that you are likely to encounter some of the stranger species in creation. Spend time contemplating the creator's exuberance and pizzazz until your imagination and spirit is saturated with wonder.

Hope

Nature's Instruction for Anticipating New Beginnings

"HOPE SPRINGS ETERNAL IN THE HUMAN BREAST," Alexander Pope once quipped. But all around us are the signs of abandoned hope. The normalization of violence, the acceptance of environmental degradation, the tolerance of gross economic inequities, and the abandonment of a belief in justice, all stand as glaring reminders of a collective loss of hope in our world.

Philosophers and thinkers throughout the ages have debated the nature of hope. Nietzsche called hope "the worst of all evils, because it prolongs the torments of men." To Shakespeare, hope, though elusive, was an ennobling virtue:

> *True hope is swift and flies with swallow's wings*
> *Kings it makes gods, and meaner creatures kings.*

What is in the nature of hope that leads some to see hope as an essential quality of the human spirit, while others mock it as an illusion to keep us from facing reality?

Hope is rooted in the future, in the anticipation of what is to come. In this respect, hope differs from faith. Faith is concerned with what is, hope with what will be. And because the future is so uncertain, some feel that hope can delude us, arousing desires and expectations that may never be fulfilled. Most of us, however, would agree with the eighteenth-century physician, Thomas Fuller, who said: "If it were not for hopes, the heart would break." Or, as the writer to the Hebrews described it, hope is "an anchor for the soul" (Hebrews 6:19).

Hope is the one virtue we crave in the deadness of a long winter, or through the darkness of grief, or in the depths of great pain. At such times, we realize just how fragile hope is, and how difficult it can be to keep hope alive. When hope dies, the result is despair.

The disappearance of hope from our social world may be related to our increasing estrangement from the natural world. As Hal Borland once observed:

> It is only when one is alienated from the earth and its eternal sequences that doubt takes root. Few of the pat answers and instant solutions have validity when you are dealing with the soil. *(Twelve Moons of the Year)*

The selections that follow provide images of hope drawn from the natural world. Many of these images are set in the springtime, for Nature seems to lift our hopes most in spring. The return of the birds, new sprouts breaking up through the bleak earth, bare limbs beginning to blossom, are all signs of resurrection, of the renewal of life. Spring is the season of Easter, the time for rebirth.

One of the deepest yearnings of the human spirit is the longing for immortality. St. Peter explains that God "has given us new birth into a living hope through the resurrection of Jesus Christ from the dead" (1 Peter 1:3). For Christians, hope is ultimately centered in the resurrection of Jesus and in the expectation of our own resurrection.

At the same time, Christians have sometimes been criticized for being "so heavenly minded, they are no earthly good." Historically, the church has not provided a clear voice of hope to those experiencing the despair of poverty, broken relationships, political oppression, domestic abuse, addictions, etc. We proclaim our great hope for the world to come, but have offered very little hope for this present world.

What difference does the presence of hope make in our lives?

First, hope is a virtue that should enable us not merely to endure; it should make us doers as well as dreamers. In one of the following selections, Phillip Keller describes how hope is awakened by the return of the first redwing blackbird, which reminds him of the presence of Christ in the world. But the gallant redwing also prompts him to wonder how his own life could bring the same sort of arresting cheer and hope to a drab social landscape.

Second, hope nourishes faith. Because hope is secondary to faith, as St. Thomas Aquinas explained, faith can remain after the loss of hope—one who despairs is not necessarily faithless. But Aquinas further notes that faith provides the object and the basis of hope. Hope is not an empty dream, as some insist, but is firmly anchored in recognizing what is, and what has been done for us. St. Paul writes: "He who began a good work in you will carry it on to completion until the day of Christ Jesus" (Philippians 1:6). For Christians, the good work that was begun provides the basis for hope; and hope for that completion in turn strengthens our faith in what God has begun.

In the previous chapter, we saw that Henry David Thoreau understood the interaction of faith and hope apart from theological jargon or dogma. Beginning his masterpiece, *Walden,* with some bold, startling observations of despair ("The mass of men lead lives of quiet desperation"), he ended the book with a story of hope and faith, the story of a bug being hatched out of a table by the heat of an urn. "Who does not feel his faith in a resurrection and immortality strengthened by hearing of this?" he exclaims.

Hope, finally, awakens us to prayer, just as prayer sustains hope. Josef Pieper once noted: "Prayer is the expression and proclamation of hope" *(The Four Cardinal Virtues).* Prayer is implicit in so many of the following selections: in Laura Lee Davidson's response to the breathtaking molting of the dragonflies; or in Kathleen

Norris' description of the farming people of South Dakota who, in the dry heat of mid-July, peer into a grave, looking for a sign of hope; or in Mechtild of Magdeburg's image of the soul, rising on its wings of longing up to God.

Nowhere is the connection between hope and prayer more beautifully demonstrated than in the example of Emily Dickinson, who extracted so many spiritual gems from nature. In one poem included in this chapter, she observes the delayed blooming of gentian in late autumn, long after the roses have faded and just before the frosts arrive, and is prompted to ask: "Creator–shall I–bloom?" Virtually unknown and unpublished at the time of her death, she is now universally regarded as one of America's greatest poets. We can now see that her faint prayer, driven by hope, was answered far beyond her wildest expectations.

Here, then, are some expressions of those who, in considering creation, found images of hope, and gave hope words.

Hope

Is not the lark companion of the spring?
And should not Hope—that skylark of the heart—
Bear, with her sunny song, Youth company?
Still is its sweetest music poured for love;
And that is not for me; yet will I love,
And hope, though only for her praise and tears;
And they will make the laurel's cold bright leaves
Sweet as the tender myrtle.

LETITIA ELIZABETH LANDON

Known familiarly as L.E.L., Letitia Elizabeth Landon (1802–38) was one of the most popular British writers in the early nineteenth century. She lived most of her brief life in
London, where she supported herself and her family through her prolific output of novels, poems, reviews, and sketches. In 1838, she married George Maclean and moved to West
Africa where she died mysteriously a few weeks after her arrival.

First Redwings

A short distance from my home on the hill, about a mile as the ospreys fly, there is a small marsh. It is only about two acres in area. It lies quietly, tucked in close against high clay cliffs, ringed with brown and golden-stalked bulrushes. Here the mallards love to come and nest. Here the ospreys love to fish in the still waters. Here the redwing blackbirds love to sing in the spring.

But spring has been slow to come this year. Already it is long past the time when the golden buttercups burst from the brown earth on the south slopes. The hills are still cold and drab and dense. The whole world is waiting for winter to leave. The countryside seems spent with the severity of so much ice and snow.

But there is hope in the air.

Three days ago I passed the gentle marsh, so brown, so brittle, and so beaten back by winter winds. And there, there, clinging bravely to a cattail stalk was a solitary, brave, bold, redwing blackbird. His jet black plumage shone bright with iridescent intensity. His scarlet shoulders trembled with their glorious red epaulettes as handsome as any army general's full-dress uniform.

He was the first redwing from the far-flung marshes of the south, the first brave bird to cross the mountain passes of the west in northern flight to find his favorite marsh beside us. He was the first to fling his wild notes into the wind and declare to all the world, "Spring is here, even if you can't see it."

In that sudden glimpse of the "little general," so utterly fearless and unafraid, my heart leaped up with joyous hope. Yes, spring was back! The birds were back! The sun was back! Even if all around seemed so stark and dark.

And the profound conviction caught up in my inner spirit. So it is, too, with our weary old world and its drab days. Christ is here. His Spirit moves amongst us. There is hope in the air. Our Father's faithfulness never falters. Life springs anew in my soul. He is here!

But a much more profound question, searching, searing, shot through my spirit as I glimpsed the gallant redwing alone in his dreary, drab surroundings. Did my presence, my life, or my coming bring similar uplift into my seared and sad society?

Was or is there something arresting, startling, or reassuring about my "just being here" that awakens onlookers to realize spring is here—to inject an element of good cheer into a social landscape of drabness and despair? Increasingly our culture is like a cold and cruel terrain, gripped by the grim vices of a realm gone wrong. Amid this ominous outlook, with so little hope, is there a sudden sparkle of spring because one of God's children is bold enough to be His redwing?

W. PHILLIP KELLER

W. Phillip Keller, the author of *A Shepherd Looks at Psalm 23* and more than thirty-five other Christian books, grew up in a missionary home in Africa. He was trained as an agronomist and currently lives in Canada. In many regions, the return of redwing blackbirds is one of the surest signs of spring. Males usually return before the females, and defend their territories vigorously.

Dragonfly Season

This is dragonfly season. Millions of them are darting through the air—great green and brown ones with a wing-spread of three to four inches; wee blue ones, like lances of sapphire light; little inch-long yellow ones, and beautiful, rusty red.

Today I spent three hours on the dock watching one make that wonderful transition from the life amphibious to the life of the air. Noon came and went, food was forgotten while that miracle unfolded there before my very eyes.

I was tying the boat, when I saw what looked like a very large spider, crawling up from the water and out on a board. It moved with such effort and seemed so weak that I was tempted to put it out of its pain. But if I have learned nothing else in all these months in the woods, I have thoroughly learned to keep hands off the processes of nature. Too often have I seen my well-meant attempts to help things along end in disaster. So I gave the creature another glance and prepared to go about my business, when I noticed a slit in its humped back, and a head with great, dull beads of eyes pushing out through the opening. Then I sat down to watch, for I realized that this was birth and not death.

Very slowly the head emerged and the eyes began to glow like lamps of emerald light. A shapeless, pulpy body came working out and two feeble legs pushed forth and began groping for a firm hold. They fastened on the board and then, little by little and ever so slowly, the whole insect struggled out, and lay weak, almost inanimate, beside the empty case that had held it prisoner so long.

Two crumpled lumps on either side began to unfurl and show as wings. The long abdomen, curled round and under, like a snail-shell, began to uncurl and change to brilliant green, while drops of clear moisture gathered on its enameled sides and dripped from its tip. The transparent membrane of the wings, now held stiffly erect, began to show rainbow colors, as they fanned slowly in the warm air, and, at last, nearly three hours after the creature had crept out of the water, the great dragon-fly stood free, beside its cast-off body lying on the dock. And

> "Because the membraned wings,
>   So wonderful, so wide,
> So sun-suffused, were things
>   Like soul and nought beside,"

certain stupendous phrases rose in my mind and kept sounding through my thoughts.

"Behold, I show you a mystery. We shall not all sleep, but we shall all be changed."

There it stood, that living jewel, growing every moment more strong, more exquisite, waiting perhaps for some trumpet call of its life. Suddenly it stiffened, the great wings shot out horizontally, and with one joyous, upward bound, away it flashed, an embodied triumph, out across the shining water, straight up into the glory of the sun.

When I came to myself I was standing a-tiptoe gazing up after it, my breath was coming in gasps and I heard my own voice saying: "It is sown in weakness, it is raised in power....Thanks be to God, which giveth us the victory."

Then, standing there under those trees, clothed in their new green and upspringing to the sky, and beside the lake, where the young ferns troop down to the water's edge, valiant little armies with banners, there came to me one of those strange flashes of understanding, that pierce for an instant the thick dullness of our minds, and give us a glimpse of the meaning of this life we live in blindness here.

I had seen those woods, all bare and dead, rise triumphant in a glorious spring. I had seen that lake grow dark and still and lie icebound through the strange sleep of winter. Its water now lay rippling in the sun.

Since my coming to Many Islands, one year ago, the Great War has broken forth, civilization has seemed to die, and the hearts of half the world have gone down into a grave.

But even to me has come the echo of the Great Voice that spoke to John, as he stood gazing on a new heaven and new earth:

"I am the beginning and the end," it said. "Behold I make all things new."

Laura Lee Davidson

Laura Lee Davidson (1870–1949) was a schoolteacher who, in 1914, decided she needed a year of rest away from the noise and confusion of Baltimore. "I have loved the woods all my life," she said; "I long to see the year go round there just once before I die." She spent a year living in a one-room cabin on an island in Canada's Lake of Many Islands. Here, she reflects upon the signifi-cance of that experience.

When Despair for the World Grows in Me

When despair for the world grows in me
and I wake in the night at the least sound
in fear of what my life and my children's lives may be,
I go and lie down where the wood drake
rests in his beauty on the water, and the great heron feeds.
I come into the peace of wild things
who do not tax their lives with forethought
of grief. I come into the presence of still water.
And I feel above me the day-blind stars
waiting with their light. For a time
I rest in the grace of the world, and am free.

WENDELL BERRY

Born in 1934, Wendell Berry is widely known as a poet, essayist, and environmentalist who practices what he preaches. His clear, prophetic voice speaks out for the importance of community, of sustainable agriculture, and of living in harmony with the natural world. "Essential wisdom accumulates in the community much as fertility builds in the soil," he believes. Berry's many books include: *The Unsettling of America: Culture and Agriculture* (1975), *The Gift of Good Land* (1981), and *What Are People For?* (1990). Wendell Berry lives on a farm in Kentucky.

Looking for a Sign of Hope

"All flesh is grass" is a hard truth, too, and it has real meaning for people who grow grass, cut it, bale it, and go out every day in winter to feed it to cows. They watch that grass turning into flesh, knowing that they in turn will eat it as beef. They can't pretend not to know that their flesh, too, is grass. And they know that grass dies, not just in the winter, but in summer's dry heat. "All flesh is grass, and its beauty is as the flower of the field." That image comes alive in the West River of Dakota, and also an image from Psalm 90 that speaks of "grass that springs up in the morning" and "by evening withers and fades."

❧

One former minister at Hope who had come from the urban East told me that her strongest memory of Hope Church was of an evening service in July. Standing in the pulpit she could see down the length of the church and out the open door to a large round hay bale catching the last rays of sunlight. "It was dark on one side and pure gold on the other," she said, "and I thought, that's a measure of the wealth here, that will help make things come out right this year."

She also told me that she couldn't imagine what was happening at the first funeral service she conducted for a member of Hope Church when, as people gathered for the graveside service, the men, some kneeling, began studying the open grave. It was early November, and someone explained that they were checking the frost and moisture levels in the ground. They were farmers and ranchers worried about a drought. They were mourners giving a good friend back to the earth. They were people of earth, looking for a sign of hope.

KATHLEEN NORRIS

South Dakota writer Kathleen Norris has occasionally served as a lay pastor at Hope Church. In this selection from her best-selling memoir *Dakota: A Spiritual Geography,* Norris writes, "I learned at Hope Church just how profoundly the activities of farming and ranching, working the land and working closely with animals, affect the way people approach matters of life and death."

Hope from the Soil and the Seasons

By late April the countryman is thinking of June and haying, of summer and the growing season, even of September and golden October. The hillside birches still show only a gauzy green haze of leaftips, the swamp maples blush with half-opened blossoms, and mornings are still frosty; but he can see corn knee-high in his newly plowed fields, oats ripening on the lower forty, strawberries ripening in the kitchen garden. Today's weather, good or bad, can't greatly change this view of the world the country man knows. Whether he is optimist or not, he has confidence in the soil and the seasons.

The closer one lives to the land, the less one distrusts time. It is only when one is alienated from the earth and its eternal sequences that doubt takes root. Few of the pat answers and instant solutions have validity when you are dealing with the soil. You see the slow but certain growth of trees, the persistence of grass, and you are aware of the tenacity of life. The earth's urgency is toward growth and renewal, and one season follows another despite man's diversions and interruptions. You can't hurry spring, and you can't interdict summer.

The countryman lives with these truths, no matter how they are phrased. He lives by them. They shape his life. So he looks about him now with confidence and with hope. Another growing season is at hand, deliberate as always, and he lays his plans, not for tomorrow but for June and July and next September.

HAL BORLAND

Hal Borland (1900–78) was born in Sterling, Nebraska, and worked for many years as a journalist and writer of stories, western novels, and essays, but he preferred to think of himself as a "natural philosopher." His writing was often compared to the work of nine-teenth-century naturalist, Henry David Thoreau. Borland's columns and essays appeared in the *New York Times* from the 1930s until his death.

Eagle Poem

To pray you open your whole self
To sky, to earth, to sun, to moon
To one whole voice that is you.
And know there is more
That you can't see, can't hear
Can't know except in moments
Steadily growing, and in languages
That aren't always sound but other
Circles of motion.
Like eagle that Sunday morning
Over Salt River. Circled in blue sky
In wind, swept our hearts clean
With sacred wings.
We see you, see ourselves and know
That we must take the utmost care
And kindness in all things.
Breathe in, knowing we are made of
All this, and breathe, knowing
We are truly blessed because we
Were born, and die soon, within a
True circle of motion,
Like eagle rounding out the morning
Inside us.
We pray that it will be done
In beauty.
In beauty.

JOY HARJO

Born in 1951 in Tulsa, Oklahoma, Joy Harjo has received numerous awards for her poetry, including the American Indian Distinguished Achievement Award (1990), the American Book Award (1991), and the Lifetime Achievement Award, Native Writers' Circle of America (1998).

On Wings of Longing

When a bird remains long on the ground it thereby weakens its wings and its feathers grow heavy. Then it rises, flaps its wings and swings itself up till it takes to the air and glides into flight. The longer it flies, the more blissfully it soars, refreshing itself, hardly alighting on the earth to rest. So it is with the soul: We must prepare ourselves in the same way if we wish to come to God. We must rise on wings of longing up to him.

MECHTILD OF MAGDEBURG

Unhappy with the lack of humiliation in her noble family in Saxony, Mechtild of Magdeburg (ca. 1210–80) fled to become a Beguine at Magdeburg, a lay sister who lived in a religious community not bound by vows. She led a life of penance and prayer, and her visions of God, published as *The Light of Godhead,* deeply influenced German medieval spirituality.

The Eagle of the Soul

There is a Catskill eagle in some souls that can alike dive down into the blackest gorges, and soar out of them again and become invisible in the sunny spaces. And even if he for ever flies within the gorge, that gorge is in the mountains; so that even in his lowest swoop the mountain eagle is still higher than other birds upon the plain, even though they soar.

HERMAN MELVILLE

Herman Melville (1819–1891) struggled throughout his life with depression and discouragement. This compelling image from *Moby Dick* suggests that even within the darkness of a deep gorge, the soul can soar.

Signs of Hope in the Winter Sea

In the sea, as on land, spring is a time for the renewal of life. During the long months of winter in the temperate zones the surface waters have been absorbing the cold. Now the heavy water begins to sink, slipping down and displacing the warmer layers below. Rich stores of minerals have been accumulating on the floor of the continental shelf—some freighted down the rivers from the lands; some derived from sea creatures that have died and whose remains have drifted down to the bottom; some from the shells that once encased a diatom, the streaming protoplasm of a radiolarian, or the transparent tissues of a pteropod. Nothing is wasted in the sea; every particle of material is used over and over again, first by one creature, then by another. And when in spring the waters are deeply stirred, the warm bottom water brings to the surface a rich supply of minerals, ready for use by new forms of life. . . .

🖋

But the symbols of hope are not lacking even in the grayness and bleakness of the winter sea. On land we know that the apparent lifelessness of winter is an illusion. Look closely at the bare branches of a tree, on which not the palest gleam of green can be discerned. Yet, spaced along each branch are the leaf buds, all the spring's magic of swelling green concealed and safely preserved under the insulating, overlapping layers. . . . Dig down through the snow into the earth. There are the eggs of next summer's grasshoppers; there are the dormant seeds from which will come the grass, the herb, the oak tree.

So, too, the lifelessness, the hopelessness, the despair of the winter sea are an illusion. Everywhere are the assurances that the cycle has come to the full, containing the means of its own renewal. There is the promise of a new spring in the very iciness of the winter sea, in the chilling of the water, which must, before many weeks, become so heavy that it will plunge downward, precipitating the overturn that is the first act in the drama of spring. There is the promise of new life in the small plantlike things that cling to the rocks of the underlying bottom, the almost formless polyps from which, in spring, a new generation of jellyfish will bud off and rise into the surface waters.

RACHEL CARSON

Rachel Carson (1907–64), a marine biologist, wrote this passage on hope in her best-selling book, *The Sea around Us* (1951).

A Story of Hope

In the early nineteenth century, Timothy Dwight, a Boston cleric, reported that a 240-mile journey from his home to New York City passed no more than twenty miles of forest; surveying the changes wrought by farmers and loggers in New Hampshire he wrote: "The forests are not only cut down, but there appears little reason to hope they will ever grow again."

Less than two centuries later, and despite great increases in population, 90 percent of New Hampshire is covered by forest. Vermont has gone from 35 percent woods in 1850 to 80 percent today, and even Massachusetts has seen its woodlands rebound to the point where they cover nearly two-thirds of the commonwealth. This process, which began as the fertile fields of the Midwest replaced the cold and rocky pastures of the East, has not yet run its course; forest cover in New York State, for instance, continued to grow by more than a million acres a decade through 1980. In sum, says Douglas MacCleery of the U.S. Department of Agriculture, "the forest and farmland landscape of the Appalachians, as well as many other parts of the East and South, has come full circle. By the 1960s and 1970s, the pattern of forest, field and pasture was similar to that prior to 1800, its appearance much like it must have been prior to the American Revolution."

If you're looking for hope, this unintentional and mostly unnoticed renewal represents the great environmental story of the United States—in some ways, of the whole world. Here, not far from where "suburb" and "megalopolis" were added to the world's vocabulary, an explosion of green is under way. In the therapeutic terms of the moment, this is the first region on earth to hit bottom and then, blessed with adequate rainfall, go into recovery. In his journal Thoreau listed the species gone from Concord by the middle of the nineteenth century: bear, moose, deer, porcupine, wolf, beaver, turkey. In 1989 environmental police had to kill a moose that had taken up residence on the median strip of Route 128, "America's Computer Highway," near Concord. "We've never been faced with a moose ten miles from Boston," said one game warden, who donated the animal's carcass to a Salvation Army soup kitchen. Further north, 316 moose were killed in collisions with cars in 1987 in Maine—in a state where, according to one eighteenth-century historian, "it is rare to see one at the present time." The same stories can be told about deer (there was no deer season in Vermont from 1865 to 1897, because there were no deer) or beaver or coyote or bear. "The shad, the eagle, and the turkey are returning," a team of Abenaki Indians wrote recently in a book about the northern forest. "The bear, the moose, and many of our other relations have shown us the ways of life, and have taught us and sustained us. Their life and our life are one." Present tense.

❧

So I want to tell this story of hope. Not because the East is a paradise now, but precisely because it isn't. Our woods will never again be forest primeval: they will forever be affected by our economies and habits, by our care or carelessness. Wilderness—in its truest sense, of places totally separated from human influence —is extinguished, here as everywhere else. But I'm done mourning. Innocence gone, we need to work wisely to build societies that allow natural recovery, that let the rest of creation begin, however tentatively, to flourish once more. And we need to do it quickly, for the recovery even of the East is tentative and uncertain. Every kind of human threat imperils this new nature, as we shall soon see. For the moment, though, I want this region to stand for the most bottom-line kind of hope. . . .

BILL McKIBBEN

Born in 1960, Bill McKibben was educated at Harvard and now lives in the Adirondack Mountains. As a Christian, McKibben writes about the impact of consumerism on the global environment. His writing has been widely respected for its prophetic insight, its engaging style and its pervasive tone of hope. His books include *The End of Nature* (1989), *The Comforting Whirlwind: God, Job, and the Scale of Creation* (1994), and *Hope, Human and Wild* (1995), from which this selection was taken.

To Live in the Mercy of God

To lie back under the tallest
oldest trees. How far the stems
rise, rise
    before ribs of shelter
       open!

To live in the mercy of God. The complete
sentence too adequate, has no give.
Awe, not comfort. Stone, elbows of
stony wood beneath lenient
moss bed.

And awe suddenly
passing beyond itself. Becomes
a form of comfort.
      Becomes the steady
   air you glide on, arms
stretched like the wings of flying foxes.
To hear the multiple silence
of trees, the rainy
forest depths of their listening.

To float, upheld,
   as salt water
would hold you.
      once you dared.

DENISE LEVERTOV

"If we are to survive the disasters that threaten," claimed Christian poet Denise Levertov (1923–97), "we need tremendous transformations of imaginative energy. We need life, and abundantly—we need poems of the spirit."

God Made a Little Gentian

God made a little Gentian–
It tried–to be a Rose–
And failed–and all the Summer laughed–
But just before the Snows

There rose a Purple Creature–
That ravished all the Hill–
And Summer hid her Forehead–
And Mockery–was still–

The Frosts were her condition–
The Tyrian would not come
Until the North–invoke it–
Creator–Shall I–bloom?

EMILY DICKINSON

Emily Dickinson (1830–86) spent nearly all her life in her father's house in Amherst, Massachusetts, virtually unknown. Only a handful of her nearly 2,000 poems were published in her lifetime—all anonymously. She is now widely regarded as one of America's greatest poets. In this poem, the example of the late-blooming gentian plant provides a hopeful context for her final question, which is a prayer.

A Field of Crickets

Nothing, short of the scent of lilacs in early spring, can stir the memory like the sound of a field of crickets on a warm September evening, while bats wheel and dart silently overhead in the twilight.

Let me tell you what I've learned about field crickets from Edwin Way Teale. From the time they hatch in the spring, these insects will eat just about anything they find. Their powerful jaws have been known to ruin gloves or a bandanna left in the field overnight. As they eat, almost constantly, their body swells against the inflexible, chitin shell until it splits open and they step out. Again and again they molt, growing larger and larger, until their final molt in late summer when they acquire wings.

Both male and female crickets get wings, but only the male has the raspy little structures which produce the familiar chirping sound when they rub one wing against another. It's an irresistible sexual serenade.

The female cricket can be recognized by her ovipositor, a long needle which trails behind her, nearly as long as her body. Once mated, she thrusts this needle into the earth and deposits her eggs, sometimes hundreds of eggs, one at a time, each about the size of the font I use on my computer, twelve to the inch.

These eggs will lie buried all winter. She will never see them hatch. The first freeze, soon to descend, will kill her, will kill the males who chirp so lustily now, will kill them all. The field, overnight, will turn silent.

As for the eggs, they'll need the freeze. If you dig them up and take them into the warmth, they simply won't hatch. They must endure the long grip of winter.

Observing the crickets in my field, I think of the cricket's ovipositor as a natural metaphor for the pen. I've spent the summer in my field, voraciously consuming whatever I could find—mostly books. Hundreds of books on all sorts of topics. I've gorged myself and split my skin open, again and again, casting aside one hard shell after another. I've acquired wings, thin fragile things. I've basked in the sun. I've leaped about and serenaded my mate. And (if you'll allow me to appropriate both sexes of cricket), I've been thrusting my egg-sized letters into the earth with my pen, with my pencil, with the keys of my computer—one by one, hundreds of them each day. These months have been closer to heaven than I've known. Never have I felt such joy.

But the fall is approaching. And the cold will descend. It always does. The rigors of the academic year will grip me, slowly at first, with a numbing chill, then suddenly, the hard freeze. And overnight, the summer life I've known will be extinguished.

I have to believe that these eggs I've been thrusting into the soil of these pages need this hard time of dormancy, too. Winter is integral to the cycle of seasons, and I'll try to welcome it as an indispensable part of the writing life as well. But I'm looking for spring. I live in the hope of resurrection.

THOMAS BECKNELL

Thomas Becknell wrote this meditation in late summer while working on this book.

Practicing the Virtue of Hope

1. Birds, for many, provide images of hope. "Hope is the things with feathers," Emily Dickinson quipped, "that perches in the soul." Notice the birds in your surroundings, and identify one bird whose presence lifts your spirits. Find out as much as you can about that bird—its habits of nesting and mating, its range, its song, etc. Make this bird a symbol of your inner life and yearnings.

2. Phillip Keller described the return of the redwings as a sign of hope. Consult a field guide to birds and learn which birds migrate to and from your region. Depending on the season, observe the arrival and departure of a particular species. Be alert, too, for those species passing through on their migration routes.

3. Over the course of a season—any season—chart the changes you see occurring in nature. Keep a daily record of all the details you observe. Try to see even the slightest changes—in the weather, in the trees, in the sounds of the insects, as new beginnings.

4. In his letter to the Philippians, St. Paul expresses confidence that "he who began a good work in you will carry it on to completion until the day of Christ Jesus" (1:6). Consider some "good work" that was begun in your life, even if it seems unfinished or abandoned. Using St. Paul's prayer of confidence, trust that God will, in time, carry on this good thing to a joyful completion.

5. Consider the late-blooming plants in your region, such as the gentian Emily Dickinson described. During the summer, note their plainness in contrast to other blooming plants; at the same time anticipate their impending beauty.

6. When despair for the world grows in Wendell Berry, he goes where the wood drake rests and the great heron feeds. Identify a spot that comforts you in a similar way. Go there deliberately and frequently, with no other purpose than to rest and to be free.

7. Bill McKibben tells a story of hope about the restoration of forest in New England. "I want this region to stand for the most bottom-line kind of hope," he says. Identify a blighted area near you that is in the process of being restored. Let this place stand for a "bottom-line kind of hope" for you. If possible, find a way to participate in the process of renewal.

Charity

Nature's Instruction
for Living through Love

NEAR THE END OF AMERICA'S BLOODY CIVIL WAR, a weary President Lincoln urged the people of the United States to get on with the task of healing the nation's wounds. "With malice toward none, with charity for all," he gently encouraged.

Americans like to consider themselves a charitable people. But in the decades following the Civil War, as the nation rebuilt and expanded, industrialism took hold and profoundly altered our concept of charity. Vast chasms opened up between those with newly acquired wealth and those without, between capital and labor, between rich and poor. Charity, as such, became part of an attempt to bridge those chasms.

Few have given more money to charity than the nineteenth-century philanthropist, Andrew Carnegie; but his concept of charity was driven by the ideology of social Darwinism, not by the social gospel. A believer in the "survival of the fittest," Carnegie felt that the changes brought about by industrial capitalism were good for the human race, however hard they might be for the individual. The person of wealth, he maintained, had a responsibility to extend charity to those less fortunate—but not to all. "In bestowing charity, the main consideration should be to help those who will help themselves," he wrote in *The Gospel of Wealth* (1889). "Neither the individual nor the race is improved by alms-giving."

Charitable giving in America today approaches 200 billion dollars each year. Yet even as we give generously, we remain conflicted about the idea of charity itself. Sociologist David Wagner calls charity America's "glorifying myth," arguing that significant social changes are not produced through philanthropy. "America's 'virtue talk' has a great deal to do with obscuring how little we as Americans actually do for people who find themselves in adverse circumstances," he says in *What's Love Got to Do with It? A Critical Look at American Charity*.

Those who receive it dislike the word "charity," for it seems cold and impersonal. Those who give it avoid using the word "love." Yet love has everything to do with genuine charity.

"If I give all I possess to the poor," wrote St. Paul in 1 Corinthians 13, "but have not love (charity), I gain nothing." Charity is not defined by the money we give. Rather, as Paul explains in that famous chapter, "Love is patient, love is kind. It does not envy, it does not boast, it is not proud. It is not rude, it is not self-seeking. . . ."

Love is, fundamentally, that desire for another to live. Love is the presence of God in the world, the motive force of all life, the greatest power in creation. Love finds its ultimate expression, according to Jesus, in laying down one's life for one's friends. "God so loved the world," we are told.

But the truth is, many find it harder and harder to see love in our world. Seldom do we witness the sort of patience and kindness and lack of self-interest that St. Paul describes. Rarely does one lay down one's life for another.

Yet the reminders of love permeate the natural world, and the writers in this chapter help us to see it. "Creation," Thomas Merton writes in his introduction to Ernesto Cardenal's book *To Live Is to Love,* "could teach man how to love if only he were willing to accept its teaching. Life as such is love, and if it is lived in truth, it teaches us to love." How can nature teach us to love? And how do we accept its teachings?

Nature, above all, desires life to continue. Elaborate rituals of courtship and mating, the sexual serenades of crickets and katydids, profligate spillings of pollen and seeds, the endless process of birth and growth and mutation and evolution. "Urge and urge and urge," wrote poet Walt Whitman. "Always the procreant urge of the world." To be sure, there is a tremendous sexual energy in nature, which Elvis Chavarría celebrates in this chapter. There is an extravagance, a vast prodigality in nature.

"All things love each other," wrote Ernesto Cardenal in his meditations on love and spirituality. "Everything in nature seeks to transcend its own limitations, to go beyond the barriers of its individuality, to meet with a *thou* to which it can give itself." This is not to say that plants and animals love as humans love, for they simply live according to their nature, without reflection. Nature, in its total embrace, through all of its complex interconnections, is one vast expression of love because it yearns to surrender to something beyond itself. St. Paul put it this way in his epistle to the Romans, "The whole creation has been groaning as in the pains of childbirth right up to the present time" (8:22).

The selections that follow bear witness to love's presence in creation. There are the biologists who open our eyes, and show me that nature is not "red in tooth and claw," as some have taught. Edward O. Wilson, the prominent Harvard biologist, shows us that altruism among animals is natural and inspiring. Wolves, explains Lois Crisler, have what it takes to live together in peace. And botanist Fritz Went explains how, among plants, the cooperative principle is stronger than the competitive one.

There is something about gardening that makes one contemplate love, as Ruth Goring does while pulling weeds. Poet Abbie Huston Evans likens love to columbine, and Mona Van Duyn ponders the tremendous and fearful capacity of "love's gibberellic wish" in her passionate prayer of a gardener.

Texas naturalist Roy Bedichek tells of a snowy egret that once descended from the blue sky to spend a night with dung-scratching chickens in a farmyard. It's a wondrous picture of nature's impulse toward love; but Bedichek also trusts the larger evocative power of the image: "The details of this evidence of a yearning for his kind are so quieting," muses Bedichek, "the folding of the egret's wings is so suggestive...." So, too, divine Love once descended from the heavens, folded its wings and chose to "roost" on earth among humans.

The Vine

Love is quaint like columbine,
Queer and new like irises
Among moon-faced flowers; a vine
All original, like these.

And it matters not a whit what it grows on, I am told;
An old shed will do for it,
Or a pillar cased in gold.

So it have, till it be grown,
Something for a trellis,—good!
Old love can climb round its own
Twisted honeysuckle wood.

ABBIE HUSTON EVANS

Abbie Huston Evans (1881–1983) grew up in Maine, the daughter of a Congregational minister, and was educated at Radcliffe. When she taught Sunday school in her father's church, one of her pupils was Edna St. Vincent Millay, who later wrote the introduction for Evans' first book of poems, *Outcrop* (1928). Millay admired the rugged beauty of Abbie Huston Evans' poetry, likening it to "the fragrance of some sturdy roadside weed which one has known since childhood without ever having guessed that it smelled at all."

I Would Be for You Rain

I would be for you rain,
yet, might bring into your
life, again, the storm;
summer days exact their dues:
troubled skies bring earth greener
hues. Lightning flashes through
the heavy air, rending it with
blinding light and thunderous
swells which press against the
inner drums of my still ears.

Have you forgotten
the grace of having wetness
rain about your face, of
watching greenness sprout,
bursting through the earth
beneath your mudcaked feet?

And for as far as the eye
can see lush fields abound,
and rainbows span the distant
hills.

I would be for you rain;
insistent, persistent, yet
intermittent. Too much
would swell the nearby waters,
flood your fruitladen fields,
laying them to waste, and,
drought has kinder hands.

Life stirs to be born again.
The waters usher in flowers
and grain. I would be for you
rain.

SARAH WEBSTER FABIO

"In love we put caring on the line," wrote Sarah Webster Fabio (1928–79) in her foreword to *My Own Thing* (1973), a volume that celebrates love and includes this beautiful poem. Fabio received her education at Fisk University. She was a leader in bringing African American Studies into colleges and universities. Fabio taught at various institutions and read her work widely throughout the United States. She published sevaral albums, as well as various collections of her poetry.

To Live is to Love

All things love each other. All nature is oriental toward a *thou*. All beings that are alive are in communion with each other. All plants, all animals, all beings are fraternally united by the phenomenon of mimesis. There are insects which mimic flowers and flowers which act like insects, animals which resemble water or rocks or desert sand or snow or woodland or certain other animals. And thus all beings love each other or feed each other, and all are united in a gigantic process of birth and growth and reproduction and death. In nature everything undergoes mutation, transformation and change, everything embraces, caresses and kisses. And the laws which rule all animate beings and to which inert nature, too, obeys (for nature, too, is alive and animated by a life that is imperceptible to us) are variants of the one law of love. All physical phenomena are likewise manifestations of the identical phenomenon of love. The cohesion of a snowflake and the explosion of a "nova," the tumble-bug that clings to a heap of dung, and the lover who embraces his beloved, manifest the same phenomenon of love. Everything in nature seeks to transcend its own limitations, to go beyond the barriers of its individuality, to meet with a *thou* to which it can give itself, an "other" into which it can transform itself. The laws of thermodynamics and electrodynamics, the laws of the propulsion of light, and the universal law of gravity, are all manifestations of the one law of Love. Everything in nature is incomplete, and everything therefore is self-giving and embrace, and all beings are in their innermost essence and in the deepest mysterious ground of their existence hunger and thirst for love.

ERNESTO CARDENAL

Born in Nicaragua in 1925, Ernesto Cardenal is an internationally known poet who is also recognized as a strong voice for social justice. Cardenal was educated at the University of Mexico and Columbia University. After his conversion to Christianity, he studied with the Trappist monk, Thomas Merton, at Gethsemani, Kentucky, where he composed this meditation. In 1965, Cardenal was ordained as a Roman Catholic priest. Back in his native Nicaragua, Cardenal developed a more radical understanding of Christianity, actively supporting the revolution against the dictator, Samoza. After the revolution, Cardenal was appointed Minister of Culture. He continues to make his home in Nicaragua.

Pulling Weeds

For me, weeding a garden area is a perfect sabbath activity. (For a farmer it probably wouldn't be.) Today is Sunday, and I spent nearly six hours of the afternoon and early evening pulling weeds in an enclosed area of my backyard. Dozens of Canadian thistles—invasive nonnative plants—had to be pulled up very carefully, so as not to leave too many roots in the ground or tiny sharp thorns in my skin. I wonder how many hundreds of other weeds I pulled up. There were a few dandelions, but the vast majority of extricated plants were of two species whose names I do not know.

I thought about the thorns and thistles of Genesis 3, the land's response to human sin. Though this piece of earth and I still suffer sin's long-term, complex effects, Jesus' cross means that we are no longer bound by the ancient curse. My task is to befriend my yard—care for it, listen to it, try to decipher its messages.

Like the acting out of a grieving child, the proliferation of these weeds speaks to me of the land's distress. The native plants of the prairie are no longer here to put nutrients back in the soil and trace deep pathways for rain with their intricate roots. I pray for this dirt and its creatures, and dream of eventually making a tiny prairie park here.

I also thought about love. Pulling weeds is inflicting death—that doesn't seem very loving. But the great mystics tell us that "the way of denial" as well as "the way of affirmation" draws the soul near to God.

Some of the major loves of my life have involved significant denials, the uprooting of initially attractive growths that proved to be invasive nonnatives. And some deaths must be undertaken over and over again. We die daily.

"Virtue seen from below looks like nothing but sheer loss" (Iris Murdoch).

But the point is love. Each excruciating denial carried out in love and wisdom opens the way to an exquisite yes. Jesus' death was a seed: though he was locked underground, apparently defeated, he rose and opened the way to the whole world's resurrection. One meaning of virtue, remember, is "power."

RUTH GORING

Ruth Goring is the editor of *Target Earth* **magazine, affiliated with the Christian Environmental Association, and published with the purpose to call Christians "to love God, serve people, and care for all creation."**

Nature's Extravagance

There is no enough in nature. It is one vast prodigality. It is a feast. There is no economy: it is all one immense extravagance. It is all giving, giving, giving: no saving, no penury; a golden shower of good things is forever descending. I love beyond all things to contemplate this indescribable lavishness— I would it could be introduced into our human life....

A man has a hundred thousand pounds: he eats and drinks and pleases his little whims— likely enough quite innocent little whims— but he never gives to a friend, or a relation; never assists, does nothing with it. This is commercially right, but it is not the buttercups in the golden mead; it is not the grain of wheat that yielded forty times. It is not according to the exemplar of nature. Therefore I say that although I admit all attempts to adjust possessions have been and for the age at least must prove failures, yet my feeling remains the same. Thrift, economy, accumulation of wealth, are inventions; they are not nature. As there are more than enough buttercups in this single meadow for the pleasure of all the children in the hamlet, so too it is a fact, a very stubborn fact, that there is more than enough food in the world for all its human children....

Thrift and economy and accumulation, therefore, represent a state of things contrary to the exemplar of nature, and in individual life they destroy its beauty. There is no pleasure without waste: the banquet is a formality; the wine tasteless, unless the viands and the liquor are in prodigal quantities. Give me the lavish extravagance of the golden mead!

RICHARD JEFFERIES

Richard Jefferies (1848–87) became best known for his children's novels, *Wood Magic* (1881) and *Bevis: The Story of a Boy* (1882), set in rural England where he grew up. Among his many non-fiction writings about nature are *Nature Near London* (1883), *The Life of the Fields* (1884) and *The Open Air* (1885). Although his works are seldom read today, their influence is evident in such later British books as Kenneth Graham's *The Wind in the Willows* and Rudyard Kipling's *The Jungle Book*.

Altruism Among Animals

In sociobiology, there is a heavy emphasis on the comparison of societies of different kinds of animals and of man, not so much to draw analogies (these have often been dangerously misleading, as when aggression is compared directly in wolves and in human beings) but to devise and to test theories about the underlying hereditary basis of social behavior. With genetic evolution always in mind, sociobiologists search for the ways in which the myriad forms of social organization adapt particular species to the special opportunities and dangers encountered in their environment.

A case in point is altruism. I doubt if any higher animal, such as a hawk or a baboon, has ever deserved a Congressional Medal of Honor according to the ennobling criteria used in our society. Yet minor altruism does occur frequently, in forms instantly understandable in human terms, and is bestowed not just on off-spring but on other members of the species as well. Certain small birds—robins, thrushes, and titmice, for example—warn others of the approach of a hawk. They crouch low and emit a distinctive thin, reedy whistle. Although the warning call has acoustic properties that make it difficult to locate in space, to whistle at all seems at the very least unselfish; the caller would be wiser not to betray its presence but rather to remain silent and let someone else fall victim.

When a dolphin is harpooned or otherwise seriously injured, the typical response of the remainder of the school is to desert the area immediately. But sometimes they crowd around the stricken animal and lift it to the surface, where it is able to continue breathing air. Packs of African wild dogs, the most social of all carnivorous mammals, are organized in part by a remarkable division of labor. During the denning season some of the adults, usually led by a dominant male, are forced to leave the pups behind in order to hunt for antelopes and other prey. At least one adult, normally the mother of the litter, stays behind as a guard. When the hunters return, they regurgitate pieces of meat to all that stayed home. Even sick and crippled adults are benefited, and as a result they are able to survive longer than would be the case in less generous societies.

EDWARD O. WILSON

Born in 1929, Harvard biologist Edward O. Wilson is known for his authority on ants and for his theories of sociobiology—the biological basis for social behavior. He has received considerable attention for his belief that altruism among animals is natural, and need not be inconsistent with other theories of natural selection.

Love in the Countryside

Güises who chatter to güisas.
The praying mantis who eats her lovers.
The billing and cooing of he-dove to she-dove.
Katydids chanting all day calling their katydads.
Fireflies that light themselves up in search of their loves.
Butterflies flying along on their wedding nights.
Crickets who sing long songs so their darlings will come.
Toads who call out to those they love best.
Great rings of gnats circling above the trees.
How full the whole countryside is with love.

ELVIS CHAVARRÍA

Elvis Chavarría was a Nicaraguan peasant who lived on an island of the Solentiname archipelago at the southern end of Lake Nicaragua. In 1965, Ernesto Cardenal, newly ordained as a priest, arrived in Solentiname and began conducting intensive discussions of the Gospels with the peasants, relating the message of the gospel to their social and economic situation. In 1977, Ernesto Cardenal brought two poet friends to Solentiname to conduct poetry workshops for some of these same peasants, including Elvis Chavarría. They found themselves developing a radical understanding of Christianity. By the end of 1977, however, Elvis Chavarría had been captured by forces loyal to the dictator Samoza, and was tortured, bound, and shot. His body was not found until after the end of the revolution, July 1979. Elvis Chavarría was remembered for his calmness, his love for children, his guitar serenades, and his laughter. The güises, mentioned in the first line, refer to the Great Kiskadee, a large flycatcher with bright yellow breast and a beautiful song.

A Snowy Egret Among Chickens

So it was with a snowy egret which spent the night in a tree among the white leghorn chickens of a coastal farm not so long ago. It was just after sundown when the farmer happened to notice a white bird sailing far above in the clear sky. He came lower in downward spirals until he was circling the tree in which the white leghorns were just going to roost. Alighting on one of the topmost branches he carefully folded his wings, adjusted his plumes, and stretched out his long neck, peering down suspiciously at the company he had chosen for the night. He shifted his position several times, but finally settled down on his stilts, heronwise, neck folded in sleeping posture.

"Next morning," said the big Norwegian farmer to me, apparently delighted to find someone interested in the occurrence, "the chickens flew down to the ground and the white bird flew up again into the sky."

This incident has stayed in my memory for months. I sometimes resort to it in bed when I can't go to sleep. The vision of that bird, the beauty of whose plumes fifty years ago spread a fierce rivalry among all the best-dressed women of the world—the picture of this, the most delicate and lovely of all the egrets, sailing down out of the blue sky to spend the night in a tree with dung-scratching fowls of the farmyard, and, come dawn, taking off again—really, the details of this evidence of a yearning for his kind are so quieting, the folding of the egret's wings is so suggestive, and the whole idyl is so clothed in sedative colors, white and blue, that I usually lose consciousness just as the bird disappears into the depths of the clear morning sky. I recommend it to others troubled with insomnia.

ROY BEDICHEK

Roy Bedichek (1878–1959) developed a lifelong love for the land and for literature from his parents who were teachers as well as farmers. Roy Bedichek graduated from the University of Texas in 1903, taught high school, then returned to the University where he held various positions. In 1947, at the age of 69, he published his first book, *Adventures with a Texas Naturalist*. The following year he retired and began work on a second book. This description of an egret roosting among chickens is richly suggestive, and may remind us of the divine descending to "roost" on earth among humans.

The Lesson

My cot was down by a cypress grove,
    And I sat by my window the whole night long,
And heard well up from the deep dark wood
    A mocking-bird's passionate song.

And I thought of myself so sad and lone,
    And my life's cold winter that knew no spring;
Of my mind so weary and sick and wild,
    Of my heart too sad to sing.

But e'en as I listened the mockingbird's song,
    A thought stole into my saddened heart,
And I said, "I can cheer some other soul
    By a carol's simple art."

For oft from the darkness of heart and lives
    Come songs that brim with joy and light,
As out of the gloom of the cypress grove
    The mocking-bird sings at night.

So I sang a lay for a brother's ear
    In a strain to soothe his bleeding heart,
And he smiled at the sound of my voice and lyre,
    Though mine was a feeble art.

But at his smile I smiled in turn,
    And into my soul there came a ray:
In trying to soothe another's woes
    Mine own had passed away.

PAUL LAURENCE DUNBAR

Born to former slaves in Dayton, Ohio, Paul Laurence Dunbar (1872–1906) wrote verses, often in dialect, which became enormously popular during his brief lifetime.

A Prayer

Teach me, Father, how to go
Softly as the grasses grow;
Hush my soul to meet the shock
Of the wild world as a rock;
But my spirit, propt with power,
Make as simple as a flower.
Let the dry heart fill its cup,
Like a poppy looking up;
Let life lightly wear her crown,
Like a poppy looking down,
When its heart is filled with dew,
And its life begins anew.

Teach me, Father, how to be
Kind and patient as a tree.
Joyfully the crickets croon
Under shady oak at noon;
Beetle, on his mission bent,
Tarries in that cooling tent.
Let me, also, cheer a spot,
Hidden field or garden grot—
Place where passing souls can rest
On the way and be their best.

EDWIN MARKHAM

Edwin Markham (1852–1940) worked as a teacher, headmaster, lecturer and editor for much of his life. He became internationally famous in 1899 when, at the age of 47, he published "The Man With the Hoe," a poem inspired by Millet's painting of the same title. In 1922, President Taft invited Markham to read "Lincoln, the Man of the People" at the dedication of the Lincoln Memorial in Washington, D.C.

Living Peaceably Like Wolves

Wolves have what it takes to live together in peace.

For one thing, they communicate lavishly. By gestures—the smile, for instance—and by sounds, from the big social howls to the conversational whimpers. They even seek to control by sounds first, not by biting. A full-grown wolf will plead with you not to take his possessions. And you in turn can plead with a wolf. He glances at your eyes, desists from what displeased you and walks off as if indifferent.

They have the big three peace enablers: social observingness (that wonderful wolf attentiveness turned upon social nuances), social concern, and what we used to call feral generosity. Now we realized it was deeper than that. It is social responsibility. We were to see more of it as our wolves grew older. But already we had seen wolves, both male and female, instantly take over responsibility for feeding and protecting from us pups not their own.

Wolves will do the same for dog pups. Disgorge for them too. Our male wolf Coonie, whom we reared later, kidnapped a dog pup, not to kill but to care for. Wolves are crazy about puppies.

Also they feel concern for an animal in trouble even when they cannot do anything for it. A dog got his nose full of porcupine quills on our walk one day. All the way home the wolf Alatna hovered anxious-eyed around his face, whimpering when the dog cried in trying to tramp the quills out. The other dogs with us ran along indifferently.

A new dog was chained and crying. All night a wolf stayed near him, whimpering a little when he cried. The other dogs slept.

A young dog wandered off, on our daily walk. The wolf with us ran to me, cried up to my face, then standing beside me looked searchingly around, call-howling again and again. When the dog sauntered into view the wolf bounded to him and kissed him, overjoyed.

Incidentally, as to this unexpected business of losing each other, wolves are gazehounds and will eagerly overpass a trail and lose it. When Trigger and Tootch ran a caribou, the dog followed the zigzag scent trail. The wolf raised his head and ran straight toward the prey.

The hardest wolf behavior for humans to fathom is the "species quality." The wolf is gentlehearted. Not noble, not cowardly, just nonfighting. Trigger and Lady did not defend the wolf pups from Tootch. The pups' parents did not defend them from the men stealing them from the den. The first time Alatna witnessed a dog fight she was frantically upset. She would have jumped on any innocent bystander, but she did not, as a dog would have done, join the fight; she tried to end it. She did not know what to do; she stammered, as it were, in her actions. At last, incredibly, she pulled the aggressor off by the tail! (The socially observant wolf was never to err about who started a fight.)

The gentleness of wolves is often mentioned in early American accounts—gentleness both as nonbelligerence and as limited flight reaction. Captain Lewis of the Lewis and Clark expedition said that in the neighborhood of buffalo killed by Indians they saw a great many wolves: "they were fat and extremely gentle." He added that Captain Clark killed one of them with a short staff, gentleness being, it would seem, no part of the Captain's own nature.

Gentleness may be appearing in our species. But the deadly words of Konrad Lorenz still characterize our species quality. "Latent in all mankind are the terrible drives of a very irascible ape."

It is almost as hard for us to sense our own species quality as it is to sense our species smell. We have an ape-fretfulness as well as irascibility. I caught a momentary glimpse of our species quality, so profoundly different from the species quality of wolves, the first time I returned to a city after living with wolves on the tundra. Suddenly, for just a little while, I was conscious of our species as a visitor from another planet might be conscious of it. The nervous faces; the fidgety, trifling, meaningless moves and objects; all the mincing paraphernalia of our weakly, thin-skinned, fetuslike species. I thought of the wide clean tundra, hundreds of miles of it, and the baggageless, purposeful, radiant pups that ranged that tundra with us.

In a reasonable world these peaceful predators would be the most cherished object of study by our race, trying to unlearn war. Why then do people hate wolves and seek to exterminate them? Probably for the same reasons as they do people.

LOIS CRISLER

Lois Crisler (1896–1971) and her husband Herb were both experienced nature photographers when they received an assignment from Walt Disney to film wolves, caribou, and wildlife in Alaska. Crisler wrote of these experiences in the 1950s in her books, *Arctic Wild* and *Captive Wild*.

Cooperation of Plants

Remarkably enough, plants have few weapons or defense mechanisms with which they attack or fend off other plants. This does not mean that they have to submit to any parasite which comes near them: all have more or less effective structures or reactions capable of preventing fungus or bacterium from penetrating and attacking them. It is usually the plants struggling under poor growing conditions in places where they should not be which are attacked most by pests and diseases; plants in favorable circumstances are much less beset by insects and parasitic fungi.

But what are the relations between individual plants in a forest or other type of vegetation? Do they struggle with each other? Do they fight for a place in the sun? What are the decisive factors determining which one of the thousands of acorns or chestnuts produced by a single tree will ultimately replace it when it dies? Is there the same awful attrition of seedlings and young trees as there is of tadpoles or young salmon, of which many thousands hatch, but only a scant few grow up to mature?

Seeking a case of extreme competition between individual plants, I thought I had found it in the desert. When, on rare occasions, a heavy rain awakens the seeds which have been lying dormant in the desert sands during the dry years, a thousand or more seedlings may sprout on every square foot of this usually barren soil. They may be so dense that the seedling leaves cover the surface with a carpet of green. Everything I had ever read about evolution prepared me to find at such a time a jockeying for supremacy, a struggle for space and an ultimate victory of a few plants which managed to outgrow the others. And what actually happened?

All of these seedlings grew. They grew slowly, to be sure, but more than half of them got far enough in that arid habitat to form a few leaves, at least one flower and ultimately a few seeds. It was *not* a case of a few outgrowing the others and monopolizing the light, moisture and nutrients—they grew up eventually, equally sharing available space. . . . There is no violent struggle between plants, no warlike mutual killing, but a harmonious development on a share-and-share-alike basis. The cooperative principle is stronger than the competitive one. . . .

FRITZ W. WENT

Born in 1903, Fritz W. Went grew up in Holland and became a botanist, serving as professor of plant physiology at California Institute of Technology from 1933 to 1958, and later as Professor of Botany at Washington University in St. Louis.

The Gardener to His God

I pray that the great world's flowering stay as it is,
that larkspur and snapdragon keep to their ordinary size,
and bleedingheart hang in its old way, and Judas tree
stand well below oak, and old oaks color the fall sky.
For the myrtle to keep underfoot, and no rose
to send up a swollen face, I pray simply.

There is no disorder but the heart's. But if love goes leaking
outward, if shrubs take up its monstrous stalking,
all greenery is spurred, the snapping lips are overgrown,
and over oaks red hearts hang like the sun.
Deliver us from its giant gardening, from walking
all over the earth with no rest from its disproportion.

Let all flowers turn to stone before ever they begin to share
love's spaciousness, and faster, stronger, larger
grow from a sweet thought, before any daisy
turns, under love's gibberellic wish, to the day's eye.
Let all blooms take shape from cold laws, down from a cold air
let come their small grace or measurable majesty.

For in every place but love the imagination lies
in its limits. Even poems draw back from images
of that one country, on top of whose lunatic stemming
whoever finds himself there must sway and cling
until the high cold God takes pity, and it all dies
down, down into the great world's flowering.

MONA VAN DUYN

Born in 1921, Mona Van Duyn grew up in Iowa and began writing poetry secretly through grade school. She has won numerous awards for her poetry, including the Pulitzer Prize (1991). Mona Van Duyn was appointed U.S. Poet Laureate, 1992–93. Often described as a "love poet," she is known for writing intelligent, unsentimental, sophisticated poems, rich in domestic imagery. This poem, in the form of a prayer, expresses a complex, but genuine, emotional response to the tremendous and fearful capacity of love.

Practicing the Virtue of Charity

1. A minimal expression of charity might be the giving of a cup of cold water (see Matthew 10:42) What could it mean for you not only to give a cup of water, but to be "rain," as Sarah Webster Fabio portrays it in her poem?

2. Richard Jefferies observes an extravagance in nature, and wishes it could be introduced into human life. Practice such extravagance where it is not expected and in such a way that you expect nothing in return.

3. Andrew Carnegie believed that "in bestowing charity, the main consideration should be to help those who will help themselves." Read the famous chapter on charity (love) from 1 Corinthians 13. What do you think should be the "main consideration" in bestowing charity? Compose your own prescription for charity, rewriting Carnegie's prescription. Then, try putting that concept into practice.

4. For Abbie Huston Evans, "Love is quaint like columbine." Find an object from nature—besides the well-worn rose—and create your own image of what love is like. Allow that image of love guide your actions.

5. "All things love each other," wrote Ernesto Cardenal; "all beings are in their innermost essence and in the deepest mysterious ground of their existence hunger and thirst for love." Practice seeing the world from this perspective. What difference might it make in your response to others, if you perceived them, in their innermost being, hungering and thirsting for love?

6. Study the natural world, and the social world, around you. Is Fritz W. Went right when he observes, "The cooperative principle is stronger than the competitive one"? In what situations might you practice being more cooperative than competitive?

7. Here are some worthwhile books to deepen your understanding and practice of love: Roberta C. Bondi, *To Love as God Loves;* C. S. Lewis, *The Four Loves;* Martin Luther King, *Strength to Love;* M. Scott Peck, *The Road Less Travelled: A New Psychology of Love.*

Author Index

Acknowledgments

Bedichek, Roy. Excerpt from *Adventures with a Texas Naturalist* by Roy Bedichek. University of Texas Press, copyright © 1947, 1961, renewed 1989. Used with permission of University of Texas Press.

Berry, Wendell. Eexcerpt from *Openings.* (Harcourt Brace & World), copyright © 1968 by Wendell Berry. Reprinted with permission of the author.

Beston, Henry. Excerpt from *The Outermost House: A Year of Life on the Great Beach of Cape Cod,* 1928. Reprinted by permission of Kate Barnes.

Borland, Hal. Excerpt from *Twelve Moons of the Year.* Copyright © 1979 by Barbara Dodge Borland. Reprinted by permission of Fances Collin, literary agent.

Cardenal, Ernesto. Excerpt from *To Live Is to Love* by Ernesto Cardenal. Translated by Kurt Reinhardt. Copyright © 1972 by Herder and Herder. Used by permission.

Carrighar, Sally. Excerpt from *Wild Heritage,* copyright © 1965 by Sally Carrighar. Reprinted by permission of Houghton Mifflin Company. All rights reserved.

Carson, Rachel. From *The Sea around Us* by Rachel Carson, copyright 1950, 1951, 1961 by Rachel Carson renewed 1979 by Roger Christie. Used by permission of Oxford University Press, Inc.

Chavarría, Elvis. "Love in the Countryside" from *Nicaraguan Peasant Poetry from Solentiname.* Translated by David Gullette. Albuquerque, N. Mex.: West End Press, 1988. Used with permission.

Coatsworth, Elizabeth. "Poem of Praise" Reprinted with the permission of Simon & Schuster Books for Young Readers, an imprint of Simon & Schuster Children's Publishing Division from *Poems* by Elizabeth Coatsworth. Copyright © 1957 the Macmillan Company; copyright renewed © 1986 Elizabeth Coatsworth Beston.

Crisler, Lois. Pages 287–90, as submitted, from *Arctic Wild* by Lois Crisler. Copyright © 1958 by Lois Crisler. Reprinted by permission of HarperCollins Publishers, Inc.

Dickinson, Emily. Reprinted by permission of the publishers and the Trustees of Amherst College from *The Poems of Emily Dickinson,* Thomas H. Johnson, ed., Cambridge, Mass.: The Belknap Press of Harvard University Press. Copyright © 1951, 1955, 1979, by the President and Fellows of Harvard College.

Dillard, Annie. Submitted excerpt, from *Teaching a Stone to Talk* by Annie Dillard. Copyright © 1982 by Annie Dillard. Reprinted by permission of HarperCollins Publishers, Inc. Pages 134–35, 136–37 from *Pilgrim at Tinker Creek* by Annie Dillard. Copyright © 1974 by Annie Dillard. Reprinted by permission of HarperCollins Publishers, Inc.

Eiseley, Loren. Excerpt from "The Hidden Teacher" in *The Unexpected Universe,* copyright © 1969 by Loren Eiseley and renewed 1997 by John A. Eichman III. Reprinted by permission of Harcourt, Inc.

Evans, Abbie Huston. "The Vine" from *Collected Poems,* by Abbie Huston Evans, Copyright © 1950, 1952, 1953, 1956, 1960, 1961, 1966, 1970. Reprinted by permission of the University of Pittsburgh Press.

Fabio, Sarah Webster. "I Would Be for You Rain" from *My Own Thing* (1973). Used by permission of the Sarah Webster Fabio Estate.

Frost, Robert. From *The Poetry of Robert Frost* edited by Edward Connery Lathem, copyright © 1977 by Lesley Frost Ballantine, 1949, 1969 by Henry Holt and Company. Reprinted by permission of Henry Holt and Company, LLC.

Garrett, Michael. From *Walking on the Wind: Cherokee Teachings for Harmony and Balance* by Michael Garrett, published by Bear & Company, an imprint of Inner Traditions International, Rochester, VT 05767. Copyright © 1998 by Michael Garrett.

Goring, Ruth. "Praying for the Earth." Copyright © 2000 by Ruth Goring. First published in *Target Earth,* Fall 2000. Used with permission.

Gruchow, Paul. "What the Prairie Teaches Us" in *Grass Roots: The Universe of Home* (Minneapolis: Milkweed Editions, 1995). Copyright © 1995 by Paul Gruchow. Reprinted with permission from Milkweed Editions.

Harjo, Joy. "Eagle Poem" from *In Mad Love and War,* copyright © 1990 by Joy Harjo and reprinted by permission of Wesleyan University Press.

Hay, John. Excerpt from *The Undiscovered Country* by John Hay. Copyright © 1981 by John Hay. Used by permission of W. W. Norton & Company, Inc.

Hays, Edward. "Autumn Psalm of Contentment" in *Prayers for a Planetary Pilgrim.* Copyright 1988 by Forest of Peace Publishing, Inc., Leavenworth, KS 66048.

Hoff, Benjamin. Excerpt from "Cottleston Pie" from *The Tao of Pooh* by Benjamin Hoff, copyright © 1982 by Benjamin Hoff; text and illus. from *Winnie-the-Pooh* and *The House at Pooh Corner*, Copyright 1926, 1928 by E. P. Duton © 1953, 1956 by A. A. Milne. Used by permission of Dutton, a division of Penguin Putnam, Inc.

Janovy, John Jr. "Tigers and Toads" from *Back in Keith County* (St. Martin's, 1981), copyright © 1981 by John Janovy, Jr. Used by permission.

Johnson, Helene. "Fulfillment" by Helene Johnson copyright © 1928. Used by permission of Abigail McGrath.

Keller, W. Phillip. From *Outdoor Moments with God* by W. Phillip Keller. Copyright © 1994, Published by Kregel Publications, Grand Rapids, Michigan. Used by permission.

Kenyon, Jane. "The Bat," copyright © 1996 by the Estate of Jane Kenyon. Reprinted from *Otherwise: New & Selected Poems*, with the permission of Graywolf Press, Saint Paul, Minnesota.

Kingsolver, Barbara. Submitted excerpt from *High Tide in Tucson* by Barbara Kingsolver. Copyright © 1995 by Barbara Kingsolver. Reprinted by permission of HarperCollins Publishers, Inc.

Krutch, Joseph Wood. "God's Great Owl" from *The Twelve Seasons* by Joseph Wood Krutch. Copyright © 1949 by Joseph Wood Krutch. Reprinted by permission of Ayer Company Publishers. Excerpt, pp. 167–68 from *The Best of Two Worlds* by Joseph Wood Krutch. Copyright © 1953 by Joseph Wood Krutch; renewed by Marcelle Krutch. Reprinted by permission of HarperCollins, Publishers, Inc.

Lao Tzu. Excerpt from Book II, Chapter 55 and Book II, Chapter 66 of *Tao Te Ching* by Lao Tzu, translated by D. C. Lau (London: Penguin Classics, 1963). Copyright © 1963 D. C. Lau. Reproduced by permission of Penguin Books, Ltd.

Lasher, Margot. Excerpt from *And the Animals Will Teach You* by Margot Lasher. Copyright © 1996 by Margot Lasher. Reprinted by permission of the Charlotte Sheedy Literary Agency, Inc.

Leopold, Aldo. "The Community Concept" from *A Sand County Almanac; And Sketches Here and There* by Aldo Leopold, Copyright 1949, 1977 by Oxford University Press, Inc. Used by permission of Oxford University Press, Inc.

Levertov, Denise. Poems by Denise Levertov, from *Sands of the Well*, copyright ©1996 by Denise Levertov. Reprinted by permission of New Directions Publishing Group.

Lindbergh, Anne Morrow. Excerpt from *A Gift from the Sea* by Anne Morrow Lindbergh, copyright © 1955, 1975, renewed 1983 by Anne Morrow Lindbergh. Used by permission of Pantheon Books, a division of Random House, Inc.

McCormick, Adele von Rüst and Marlena Deborah McCormick. Excerpt from *Horse Sense and the Human Spirit: What Horses Can Teach Us about Trust*. Heath Communications, Inc., 1977. Copyright © 1997 by Adele von Rüst McCormick, Ph. D., and Marlena Deborah McCormick, Ph.D. Used by permission of Heath Communications, Inc.

McKibben, Bill. From *Hope, Human and Wild* by Bill McKibben. Copyright © 1995 by Bill McKibben. Used by permission of Little, Brown and Company, Inc.

Meade, Erica Helm. "The Dance of the Deer" from *Intimate Nature* by Linda Hogan, Deena Metzger, and Linda Hogan. Used by permission of Ballantine Books, a division of Random House, Inc.

Merton, Thomas. Excerpts by Thomas Merton, from *New Seeds of Contemplation*. Copyright © 1961 by The Abbey of Gethsemani, Inc. Reprinted by permission of New Directions Publishing Corp.

Moon, William Least Heat. Excerpt from *Prairyerth: A Deep Map*. Copyright © 1991 by William Least Heat Moon. Reprinted by permission of Houghton Mifflin Co. All rights reserved.

Moore, Kathleen D. Excerpt from *Riverwalking* (Lyons & Burford, 1995). Copyright © 1995 by Kathleen Dean Moore. Reprinted by special arrangement with The Lyons Press.

Morgan, Marlo. One paragraph, from *Mutant Message Down Under* by Marlo Morgan. Copyright © 1991, 1994 by Marlo Morgan. Reprinted by permission of HarperCollins Publishers, Inc.

Neihardt, John G. Excerpt from *Black Elk Speaks* by John G. Neihardt. The University of Nebraska Press, 2000. Used by permission of The University of Nebraska Press.

Norris, Kathleen. Excerpt from *Dakota* by Kathleen Norris. Copyright © 1993 by Kathleen Norris. Reprinted by permission of Houghton Mifflin Co. All rights reserved. Excerpt from *The Cloister Walk*, by Kathleen Norris, copyright © 1996 by Kathleen Norris. Used by permission of Riverhead Books, a division of Penguin Putnam, Inc.

Nowlan, Alden. "Sacrament" by Alden Nowlan. Reprinted by permission of Claudine Nowlan.

Olson, Sigurd F. Excerpt from *The Singing Wilderness* by Sigurd F. Olson. Copyright © 1956 by Sigurd F. Olson. Used by Permission of Alfred A. Knopf, a division of Random House, Inc. Excerpt from *Reflections From the North Country* by Sigurd F. Olson. Copyright © 1976 by Sigurd F. Olson. Used by permission of Alfred A. Knopf, a division of Random House Inc.

Peterson, Roger Tory. Excerpt from *Birds Over America* by Roger Tory Peterson. Copyright © 1948 by Roger Tory Peterson; renewed 1976 by Roger Tory Peterson.

Pollan, Michael. Excerpt from *Second Nature: A Gardener's Education* by Michael Pollan. Copyright © 1991 by Michael Pollan. Reprinted by permission of the author.

Rilke, Rainer Maria. "Wenn etwas mir vom Fenster fällt . . . / How surely gravity's law," from *Rilke's Book of Hours: Love Poems to God* by Rainer Maria Rilke, translated by Anita Barrows and Joanna Macy, copyright © 1996 by Anita Barrows and Joanna Macy. Used by permission of Riverhead Books, a division of Penguin Putnam, Inc.

Rogers, Pattiann. *The Dream of the Marsh Wren: Writing as Reciprocal Creation* (Minneapolis: Milkweed Edition, 1999). Copyright © 1999 by Pattiann Rogers. Reprinted with permission from Milkweed Editions.

Sanders, Scott Russell. "The Force of Spirit." Copyright © 1999 by Scott Russell Sanders; first published in *Orion*. Collected in the author's *The Force of Spirit* (Boston: Beacon Press, 2000); reprinted by permission of the author.

Sassoon, Siegfried. "December Stillness," from *Collected Poems of Siegfried Sassoon* by Siegfried Sassoon, copyright 1918, 1920, by E. P. Dutton. Copyright 1936, 1946, 1947, 1948 by Siegfried Sassoon. Used by permission of Viking Penguin, a division of Penguin Putnam, Inc.

Stalker, James. Excerpt from "Temperance" in *The Seven Deadly Sins and the Seven Cardinal Virtues* by James Stalker. Copyright © 1988 by American Tract Society. Used by permission of NavPress Publishing (www.navpress.com).

Standing Bear, Luther. Excerpt from *Land of the Spotted Eagle* by Luther Standing Bear. University of Nebraska Press, 1978. Used by permission of The University of Nebraska Press.

Thomas, Lewis. Excerpt from "Natural Man," Copyright © 1973 by The Massachusetts Medical Society, from *The Lives of a Cell* by Lewis Thomas. Used by permission of Viking Penguin, a division of Penguin Putnam, Inc.

Valles, Carlos G., S.J. Excerpt from *Courage to Be Myself* by Carlos G. Valles, S. J., Copyright © 1989 by Carlos G. Valles. Used by permission of Bantam Books, a division of Random House, Inc.

Van Duyn, Mona. "The Gardener to His God," from *A Time of Bees* by Mona Van Duyn. Copyright © 1964 by The University of North Carolina Press. Used by permission of the publisher.

Went, Fritz W. From *Life Nature Library: The Plants* by Fritz W. Went and The Editors of *Life* © 1963 Time Life, Inc.

Williams, Terry Tempest. "Redemption." From *An Unspoken Hunger* by Terry Tempest Williams, copyright © 1994 by Terry Tempest Williams. Used by permission of Pantheon Books, a division of Random House, Inc.

Wilson, Edward O. Excerpt from *The New York Times Magazine,* October 12, 1975. Reprinted by permission of The New York Times.

Wood, Douglas. Reprinted with permission from *Paddle Whispers*. Copyright © 1993 by Douglas Wood; Pfeifer Hamilton Publishers, 800-247-6789.

Wood, Nancy. From *War Cry on a Prayer Feather* by Nancy Wood, Garden City, New York: Doubleday, 1979. Used by permission.

Works Cited

Aquinas, Thomas, *Summa Theologica, I–II,* in *Basic Writings of Saint Thomas Aquinas,* volume 2, ed. Anton C. Pegis (New York: Random House, 1945).

Austin, Richard, *Baptized into Wilderness: A Christian Perspective on John Muir* (Atlanta: John Knox Press, 1987).

Baker, Richard St. Barbe, source unknown.

Chambers, Oswald, *My Utmost for His Highest* (New York: Dodd, Mead, 1935).

Cohen, Michael P., *The Pathless Way: John Muir and American Wilderness* (Madison: University of Wisconsin Press, 1984).

Hardin, Garrett, *Living within Limits: Ecology, Economics, and Population Taboos* (New York: Oxford University Press, 1993).

Levertov, Denise, *New Selected Essays* (New York: New Directions Publishing, 1992).

MacDonald, George, KSUI radio program guide, 1982; original source unknown.

Miller, Perry, *Errand into the Wilderness* (Cambridge: Harvard University Press, 1956).

Muir, John, "The Sequoia," *Our National Parks* (Boston: Houghton, Mifflin, 1901).

Pieper, Josef, *The Four Cardinal Virtues* (New York: Harcourt, Brace, and World, 1965).

Weil, Simone, *The Need for Roots,* trans. Arthur Wills (New York: Putnam, 1952).